Whispering Sands

and Other Poems

JACK SHINER

STARGAZER MUSIC & PUBLISHING

SAN FRANCISCO

1 9 8 9

Copyright 1989 by John E. Shiner

Published by:
Stargazer Music & Publishing
Post Office Box 34189
San Francisco, CA 94134-0189

Library of Congress Cataloging in Publication Data

Shiner, Jack, [date]
    Whispering Sands and Other Poems
I. Title.
PS3569.H4958W47 1989   811'.54--dc19   88-38045
ISBN 0-922224-09-9 (alk. paper) Hardcover
ISBN 0-922224-10-2 (alk. paper) Softcover

Manufactured in the United States of America
First Edition   10 9 8 7 6 5 4 3 2 1

With love to Mom and Pop

ACKNOWLEDGEMENTS

I would like to thank the following for making this collection
a reality
(In alphabetical order)

ANDY'S CAFE	A place to edit
ERIC BARTSCH	Moral Support
CAFFE ZEPHYR	A place to write and edit
GLEN GOWEN	Waking me up to the idea
ROBERT HANDWORK	Technical consultant
DUNCAN MCCALLUM	Graphics consultant
MEKONG RESTAURANT	A place to write and edit
KATHLEEN MOY	Financial consultant
RICK SHINER	Computer consultant
STARGAZER PUBLISHING	and its wonderful staff
FREDDIE WOLFORD	Photography and a push
THERESA WOO	For listening and suggestions

ABOUT THE AUTHOR

Jack Shiner (pronounced Shy-ner) was born in Royal Oak,
a suburb of Detroit. He grew up there and in Leelanau
County and Traverse City, Michigan. Since 1979 he has
lived in San Francisco, where he is employed as a systems
technician. Shiner began his self-study of poetry and
songwriting eighteen years ago. This is the first of his
work to be published.

TABLE OF CONTENTS

All this beauty I look upon
had to be pulled down
and pounded
and pressed
to become this paper I write upon
and further processed and prepared
to become the pages
these words are printed upon

From the placid beauty of the forest
to the pleasing, peaceful touch
whispering between your fingers
as you turn the page

Jack Shiner
8 October 1988
Muir Woods
Marin County, California

DAWN WILL COME

Many times I have wished that I could go to places
    where the air is thick with time and mystery
Where I'd find lost cities of great and vanished races
    who left no trails leading to their destiny
In lands that have long not seen human faces
    Lands themselves forever lost in history

And there among the hills and valleys slumbering in peace
    under brilliant blue skies sparsely clouded
I'd find a hidden city, forgotten for centuries
    that a civilization had once built and crowded
Now covered by an overgrowth of vines and ferns and trees
    Now a relic Time and Nature has left shrouded

What was this civilization at the time of its birth?
    What tales will I find of long ago?
Will I unravel many riddles of any scientific worth
    as I work my way down corridors so slow
reaching down to sift my hands
    through layers of ancient earth
        as I wonder what lies waiting down below?

I hack my way through tangled vines
    and timeworn ages, long past
        and enter into a world dark, still, and strange
Besides the dust and cobwebs
    that Time wears as a mask
        very little has actually changed
Here, where it's been ages
    since human shadows have been cast
        Where the dust of time has not been rearranged

Shuffling slowly through these halls
    where eternity softly sleeps
        Where a perpetual everlastingness looms
Where everflowing shadows
    still carefully keep
        a watchful eye over long vacant rooms
I move into the darkness
    ever cool, ever deep
        in search of the legendary tombs

With hollow, echoing footsteps
along one wall I have found
a passageway that leads me to staircases
I can see that they will take me down underground
though their destination
darkness erases
In that darkness will there be decaying matter in mounds
or antiquated pottery
and vases?

A chill comes over me
telling me I am a fool
This is the work of grave robbers and raiders
who break the seals of the past
to steal the riches and the jewels
brought by the sea merchants and traders
Sacred chambers that were built
for those who did rule
were never meant for thieves and invaders

As I reach the last step
I see in my lantern's light
not only pottery but boxes and sacks
Paintings on the walls
depicting burial rites
I see arrowheads and other artifacts
I am seeing so much
I can barely believe my sight
and a shiver goes crawling up my back

I see scenes of sacrifices
ceremonial spices
dried plants, weaponry
and other devices
I see plates of hammered gold
grand vessels of old
bracelets and rings
and treasures untold

I see words of the scribes
describing the tribes
and hunts that took place
in the vast countryside
I see words of the sages
documenting the ages

all adding to history's
uncounted pages

I stop...for a moment
to catch my breath
in this musty room
filled with gloom and death
and I think of the hands
that drew these ships
The cries and demands
that passed through the lips
of those in command
who had built this crypt
and I shudder...

I shudder as I look around at all of this
This rite of passage for one once so great
A man who ruled a world that no longer exists
A world hidden behind Time and Nature's gate
And I stand alone in History
on the edge of the abyss
without a clue as to their final fate

I wonder who and why and when and where
though I haven't yet left my rocking chair
And, someday I'll search for the how and when
but I'll read and I'll daydream until then

Yes, this is what adventures and dreams are made of
and I believe it is never too late
to try to make a dream or an adventure come true
Dawn will come
but Time
will never wait

LOVE

Love has always been
and will always be
the most puzzling pleasure
of mystery

THE SEA'S LULLABY
(To Mary Alice Shiner)

Lay back and relax
turn your face to the sun
where the roar of the waves
continues as one

A wide sandy beach
at the base of Big Blue
Its waters stretching out
far beyond your view

A lone figure walking
Bare feet touching sand
Seeking solitude and peace
in a search to understand
all things that will whisper
their way through the mind
Thoughts of the future
or times left behind

Lullaby
Lullaby
The sea breezes sigh
with the roar of the waves
and a lone seagull's cry

Lullaby
Lullaby
When sea breezes sigh
with waves and gull's cry
'tis the sea's lullaby

FORGETFULNESS

Some look at it as stupidity
or obligations being denied
When the truth is
it's only the act
of being preoccupied

LEONARDO

Leonardo DaVinci where have you gone?
  And where did you get such a mind?
A mind that would let you explore and investigate
  any little thing you could find

You touched nearly every field of study
  from architecture and drawing to botany
and made some of the first important discoveries
  in the field of anatomy

You felt that people in early paintings
  looked lumpy or as flat as a leaf
and you felt the best way to paint the Human form
  was to find out what was underneath

You drew wings for man and other vehicles
  You knew that someday Man would fly
Yes, somehow more than four centuries ago
  you knew Man would take to the sky

And you know, Leonardo, that people still wonder
  why it is the sky is blue
Why didn't I know that centuries ago
  the answer was discovered by you?

You wondered about it yourself, one day
  and you wondered of something else too
You wondered why sometimes, blue was the color
  of mountains far off in your view

You made two piles of wood
  one green and one dry
    then built of each pile a fire
Then prepared two cloths
  one black and one white
    as you watched smoke and flame rising higher

Behind the fire of dry wood
  you placed both cloths
    and the smoke in front of each was white-gray
When you placed the white cloth
  behind the fire of wet wood
    the smoke appeared to be the same way

But when you placed the black cloth
　behind the fire of wet wood
　　the white smoke appeared to be blue
The blue was the moisture
　with the black of space behind it
　　and the light of the sun passing through

So, the sky during the day is actually black
　Just as black as the sky at midnight
You saw that Nature was playing a trick on us
　The sky is blue because of moisture and light

Leonardo, did it ever cross your mind
　that centuries after your life was through
a poet would sit prying words from the air
　in an attempt to honor you?

Leonardo, I sit here far into your future
　trying to find a few words of praise
If I were to try to praise all that you've done
　I'd be sitting here writing for days

So, rather than list the fruits of your studies
　I leave it to my readers to explore
the few things that I've mentioned here
　your paintings, and so much more

Leonardo, you were so far ahead of your time
　A time that's now dusty and old
Today, we have a saying that would suit you well
　'When you were made
　　they broke the mold'

TODAY WILL NOT STAND STILL

If you really put your mind to it
　you can get hard to reach things done
But only with a positive attitude
　will you get there, in the long run

For once you say the word "can't"
　you've set yourself up to fail
Failure is a coffin
　and every "can't" is another nail

You have to believe you can do it
　Then you really have to try
And every time you make a mistake
　you cannot sit down and cry

You have to say you can do it
　You have to take a stand
You have to be able to take control
　and place your future in your hand

You have to run out of excuses
　and stop thinking of reasons why
you should let another season slip past
　or another year pass you by

You must see that today will not stand still
　There's no yesterday you can borrow
You must hope you run out of excuses
　before you run out of tomorrows

TOPANGA CANYON CHRISTMAS
(To Eric Bartsch)

At the meeting of two eternities
　I hang, suspended in space
Flexing, relaxing
　twisting, turning
　　Trying to find my place

I want to take it all with me
　Every sight
　　Every sound
　　　Everything
But I think it safe to say
　that the mysteries of the universe
　　will be waiting here for me
　　　next spring

DRAGON SMOKE

As a child
I was always curious
about manhole covers
or rather what was beneath them
What lurked under the streets?

You never saw anyone come out of them
or anything, for that matter
Only dragon smoke
and that was usually
only in the winter
I don't recall any dragons
living under the streets
in the summer
I don't know where they went then
Maybe farther north
Maybe Alaska
Maybe the Yukon
Probably not the North Pole
I don't think there are many manhole covers
at the North Pole
and only a few in the Yukon

Dragons like manhole covers
They need someplace to lurk
and with the world being civilized and all
it's tough for a dragon
to find a large enough cave
these days

Dragons don't like being pestered
by people
The only dragon I heard of
that liked people was Puff
He was a magic dragon in a song
It was popular when I was a kid
Back then
my Dad used to play the song on guitar
and sing it around the campfire
during the summer
But, that was just a dragon in a song
and he only liked one kid anyway
Nice song, though

We had a manhole cover
out in front of the house I grew up in
No dragons lived under it
There was never any dragon smoke
Not even in the winter
I used to peek in one of the holes
while allowing the second hole
to let in some light
But that little bit of light
didn't do much good
I wised up and got some matches
I would light a match
drop it in one hole
and peek into the other
Lucky for me
there were no gas mains under that one
or KA-BLAM!!!
me and that manhole cover
would have gone right through the clouds
on a magic carpet ride
to heaven

What did I see?
No dragons
I can tell you that much
It was lined with brick
and had rusty, iron rod steps
going down to the bottom
Not big enough for dragons
I could see that right away
I dropped a few more matches
and looked down there
at the stairs
the bricks
the cobwebs
the dust
and the flickering flame in the bottom
No dragons
No KA-BLAM!!!

I soon lost interest in that manhole
and never looked in it again
What was the point in it?
There were no dragons
It wasn't big enough for dragons

even if I could find one
or could lure one into the manhole
and what would I use for bait, anyway?

It wasn't big enough for a fort, either
And if it were big enough for a fort
it had one major flaw:
It was next to the curb
What if you went down there
and someone parked their car over it?
What would you do
when Mom called out for dinner?

I liked storm drains, too
They made nice gurgling sounds when it rained
You could throw leaves and stuff
in the gutter
and watch it disappear into the storm drain
Some fun

I liked to look in them, too
But I never saw anything interesting
except once
when I saw a rat run out of one
turn around
and run back in
Must have taken the wrong exit

That was the closest thing I ever saw
to a dragon coming out of the streets
But, I don't think rats can make all that smoke
Naw, no way
That's dragon smoke
I'm sure of it

Dragons live under manhole covers
and rats live in storm drains
I hear alligators do too
I guess alligators used to be a craze
I mean, live baby ones
not shoes or handbags
And when they got a little too big
Mothers or Fathers
used to give them the flush
right into the sewers

Not a very nice thing to do
But I guess some of them lived
Maybe they make the smoke

Naw, no way
That's dragon smoke
I'm sure of it

MY TAILOR'S NAME IS LEVI

My tailor's name is Levi
  and I drive a pick-up truck
    and all day long I'm working on machines
I pay my bills today
  and I'll save for tomorrow
    I still believe in living for my dreams

If I never make a million
  I won't ever die ashamed
    I'll make it down this long, hard road somehow
Nobody owes me nothin'
  and nobody can be blamed
    for trying to do all life will allow

I'd like to buy a house someday
  A handsome, little home
    but it seems that dream slips farther from my hand
The cost keeps going higher
  making it harder to own
    and just why that is I still don't understand

I still believe in this country
  and I believe in democracy
    and I believe
      that a dream can still come true
but there are things I hear
  and things I read and see
    that make me wonder what'll be left
      for me and you

WHEN YOU DON'T KNOW WHERE TO TURN

Grandma always had a dreamy look in her eyes
and Grandpa never told me any lies
I know my Mother's love will always be there
My brothers are the best friends I've ever had
and I can always trust the wisdom of my Dad
When you don't know where to turn
'tis your family who'll care

LET THE BUYER BEWARE

Let the buyer beware
It has been said
When you're using your money
always use your head
for they'll rob you blind
as they pad the bill
If you don't watch your pennies
they certainly will!

VANDALISM

A physical act of ignorance
both needless and abusing
that those with little
or no sense
somehow find amusing

ONCE BEFORE

I'm needing to smell the scent of pine
and see a million stars with my eyes
as I lay on my back on a sandy beach
and gaze at the midnight skies

I'm needing to hear the waves wash in
splashing endlessly on the shore
I'm needing to capture
a free, alive feeling
I had once before

TO INITIAL CARVERS

To those of you
with little sense
who carve initials
in trees
Carve a few initials
into your own foreheads
please!

JUST AROUND THE BEND

Half the year is already spent
and I'm not even sure
where it was it went
but there's another half
that I can lend
waiting for me
just around the bend

You can do a lot with your life
   if you'd just unplug The Tube
and realize that all of life
   is not in that little cube

There's a great big world out there
   and a bigger one in your head
Think of how long you've sat there staring
   Think of what you could be doing instead

There are four, five, or six hours
   that lay before you every night
when you could work with something that interests you
   Something that makes you feel right

You could find a new direction
   or dip a pen into your soul
Add a dream to your collection
   or take a step toward a goal

With just one hour a night
   you could teach yourself a new skill
All you need is time and patience
   practice and the will

You could learn to knit a hat
   to warm a loved one's ears
You could study to reach the goal
   of finally changing careers

You could learn to paint or draw
   or make improvements on your home
You could learn to play an instrument
   or even write a poem

There is no limit to what you can learn
   No limit to what you can find
If you give yourself the chance to try
   and open up your mind

With one hour a night, during the week
   That adds up to five
Which multiplies to twenty
   for each month that you're alive

Now, take that one and make it two
  Now, weekly, you have ten
Five hundred and twenty hours a year
  You'll learn something new by then

Now, take that two and make it three
  and weekly, you have fifteen
Are you catching on? Does it all add up?
  Do you understand what I mean?

With so much time laying at our feet
  I can't help but find it a crime
when someone says they could have been
  but didn't have the time!

OUR FIRST KISS

Thank you, so much
  for our first kiss
    Your giggles and smiles
    I always miss

The touch of your hand
  Your dreamy eyes
    Holding each other
    under rainy skies

And whether the sky
  is dark or blue
    I love to wrap
      my arms around you

All that is true
  and so is this...
    I'm looking forward
      to the next time we kiss

SAVE YOUR PENNIES

Save your pennies
and save your dimes
for they may save you
from harsher times

SITTING ON THE FRONT PORCH SWING
(IN MEMORY OF ROBERT FROST)

Sitting on the front porch swing
on a warm June afternoon
was a woman and a man
married fifty years
Their golden year
Their years were golden
Their hair was silver

She sat close to him
with her head on his shoulder
He gazed out at the field
She, down at her hands
and wedding band

With a bit of a smile
at the corners of her mouth
she asked
  "If you were to live life
    over again
      what would you ask for?"

He paused...
and looked into the sky
Then, he said
  "No aches or pains"

  "Aches or pains?!"
she exclaimed with a puzzled face
  "That's not very romantic!"

"You didn't say anything
  about romance"

"I said..." she said

"You said," he said
  "If I could live..."

"I know what I said" she said

They fell silent
She rested her head on his shoulder again
The smile returning
to the corners of her mouth

She sighed gently and said
  "Fifty years...
    Can you believe it?"

  "A couple of silly kids" he said

  "We weren't silly"
she protested
  "We were in love"

  "Yes, indeed"
he replied
  "A couple of silly kids"

She sat up in the front porch swing
and looked into his eyes
As his looked into her's
she asked
  "And what's wrong with love?"

  "Oh, love..." he replied
waving his hand as if shooing a fly
  "Love is a blessing and a curse"

  "A curse!...Oh...and how is it a curse?"

Looking into her eyes, he answered
  "You got me. Didn't you?"

Smiling
she placed her head
back on his shoulder
patted his chest with her hand
and played with the buttons on his shirt
and said
   "Oh, you're not a curse
     You're my good boy"

She smiled
looking down at her hands
He looked out into the field
making a funny face she couldn't see

   "And stop making faces" she said

   "Oh...How do you know I'm making faces?"

   "I should know you by now, I should hope"

   "I suppose you can read my mind as well"

   "Hasn't been anything exciting in there for years"
she said

She rose
and walked across the porch
He gazed at her with mock surprise
She smiled and walked in the front doorway
He smiled and leaned back
arms behind his head
sitting on the front porch swing

A LITTLE RUN DOWN

Tonight I'm feeling
a little run down
Not an ounce of energy
can be found
I'm going to spend my evening
quiet and still

Feeling a little tired
plus feeling a little cold
plus feeling a hidden feeling
of feeling a little old
all adds up to feeling
blue and ill

Heating up some rice
and chicken in a pan
I'm going to try to get
some extra sleep if I can
So I don't feel like
I'm dragging myself uphill

With orange juice in a glass
and slippers on my feet
and a little soft music
to make my night complete
(Along with a cold tablet
and a vitamin pill)

No one likes the feeling
of not feeling right
I'll sit tight
and ride this storm out tonight
with good food
some rest
some fresh-squeezed juice
and my will

THE RUSH HOUR

The level of intelligence
  always seems to drop down
everyday when the rush hour
  rushes into town
and just why that is
  is anybody's guess
People have a lot to do
  with causing their own stress

You get out on the road
  and, you know, it never fails
that you'll have some reckless wise-guy
  crawling up on your tail
And there's always some clown
  jumping the line at the light
or someone turning left
  who's decided to turn right

And then there are the girls
  who, just after dawn
are driving down the highway
  trying to put their make-up on
And what about the knuckleheads
  you wish hadn't been born
who, before the light changes
  are blowing on their horns?

Rush
  Rush
    Rush
      Hurry
        Hurry
        Hurry
Everybody's stressed out
  and starting to worry

There are cars blocking lanes
  that need to be towed
and people's minds are everywhere
  but on the road
Picking noses, combing hair
  and talking on the phone
Doesn't it seem that the expressway
  is the slowest way home?

People swearing and screaming
  Making gestures with their fingers
as the smell of exhaust fumes
  overwhelms you and lingers
People slowing down
  not sure of which exit to take
And those who don't know the difference
  between gas pedal and brake

Now, you tell me
  because I don't know
why people merge
  onto the highway so slow
And, you tell me
  because I can't guess
why they even bother calling
  the expressway 'express'

In every single city
  across this vast nation
there are accidents caused by speeding
  and by hesitation
Which, of course, causes people
  to slow down and gawk
For Pete's sake! It would be faster
  if I'd get out and walk!

Some people think we can live
  without governments or elections
when we can't even handle
  four-way stop intersections
Ah! Yes, the human animal
  becomes an animal to fear
every single week day
  when rush hour rushes near

Yes, tempers are flaring
  and temperatures are rising
when the sun peeks above
  or drops below the horizon
And if I could make one wish
  with some sort of magic power
it would be for me
  to forever and always
    miss the rush hour

SOMEDAY
(TO LIAO TSAI-LI)

Someday I'd like to go
  to Taiwan, once again
to visit some of the charming places
  where I had once been
To sit and talk with friends I met
  and one friend that I knew
before that one October
  when o'er the wide Pacific I flew
To walk the many crowded streets
  of busy, loud Taipei
To stop in New Park for awhile
  and say 'Ni Hao' along the way
Kao-Shung, Chai-Yi, Sun-Moon Lake
  Hsilo, and Ali Shan
I've many a wonderful memory
  of beautiful Taiwan

Someday I'd like to go
  to the isles of the Philippines
to bring to life the many exotic
  wonders and colorful scenes
that I have seen in many books
  and many magazines
of tall, tropical forests
  and valleys, lush and green
Of deep, clear, warm waters
  in shades of turquoise blue
Of white, sandy beaches
  reaching far beyond your view
Of red sunsets glowing
  in the warm, balmy air
Of bronze island beauties
  combing long, black, silky hair

Someday I'd like to go
  and wander in Japan
and stay there for a few weeks
  or a few months, if I can
To spend some time wandering to and fro
  on every jewel of an isle
To live in her lovely countryside
  and her cities, for awhile

To walk her streets and taste her food
   and sip her fine sake
To swim her bays and wade her streams
   and climb up Mount Fuji
To say 'domo', 'ko-ni-chi-wa'
   and 'sayonara' with a bow
would shed light on a part of a dream
   I carry with me now

Someday I'd like to go
   to visit old Germany
There's many people and places there
   that I would like to see
The Black Forest, Frankfurt, and Dusseldorf
   Munich and the town of Bonn
Where 'Der Meister' Beethoven was born
   and where his memory lives on
I'd eat bratwurst and potatoes
   with a pile of sauerkraut
Go to the many historic towns
   to browse and walk about
I'd taste their many great draught beers
   and fine liebfraumilch wine
Yes, in dear, old Germany
   I'd have a grand ol' time

Someday to old Vienna
   I would like to go
So many of the masters of music
   all lived there once, you know
Schubert, Beethoven, Haydn
   the Strauss', and Mozart
It was a cultural meeting place
   and a center for the art
Schubert played his piano
   as his friends talked and danced
Beethoven conducted his symphonies
   when he had the chance
Haydn would come around
   when not in the countryside
and it was there that Wolfgang Mozart
   that bright, young genius died

Someday I'd like to float
   down the great, wide Amazon

What a strange, mystical river
  that would be to float upon
The mysteries of the jungle
  hiding behind tall, towering trees
Danger and high adventure
  on the warm South American breeze
To see snakes slither in branches
  and hear wild birds call
To dodge through rushing rapids
  and see white, roaring waterfalls
To hear the howler monkey
  wake the jungle before dawn
Oh! What a thrill it would be
  to float down the Amazon

Someday to the Great White North
  I would like to go
To the land of the timber wolf
  and the deep, white, glistening snow
Alaska! The Northwest! The Yukon!
  and grand, wide Hudson Bay!
And farther north, where they have
  six months of night and six of day
To see the mighty polar bear
  the seals, and caribou
The Aurora Borealis
  The Eskimo and igloo
To ride behind a dogsled
  in a polar sunset's glow
Yes, to the Great White North
  someday, I'd like to go

Someday I'd like to go
  to Egypt and the Nile
to sit down and contemplate
  the pyramids for awhile
The deserts of Arabia
  The mysteries of Bombay
And stop to visit in Tibet
  and Nepal along the way
I'd like to climb Mount Everest
  just to say that I was there
See the penguins of Antartica
  and feel its frigid air

I'd like to go to China
and walk on its grand Great Wall
England, France, Australia!
I want to see it all!

Someday I'd like to sail
'round the world on the ocean blue
Climb mountains, canoe rivers
and walk through deserts too
Visit Sweden, Norway, Denmark
Leningrad, and Moscow
Hong Kong, Singapore, Bangkok
Dublin, and Glasgow
Madrid, Lisbon, Athens
Shanghai, and Rangoon
Turkey, Poland, the Netherlands
Canton, and Kowloon
From rice paddies to mountain tops
to lands, far and wide
Grab your imagination
and come along for the ride!

With imagination and a book
we can travel here and there
We can travel 'round the world
without ever leaving our chair
Spend the afternoon in Paris
Spend the night in ancient Rome
We can see the sights and the city lights
without ever leaving home
We can hear the call of the wild
and dance through the dust of ages
With imagination we can bring to life
the words upon the pages
So, reach into your soul and dream
Make a wish along the way
and say to yourself: "I'll see it all!
I'll see it all
someday!"

YOU CANNOT SAVE TIME

You cannot save time
  Once it is gone
    it is gone
  You cannot hold back the sun
as the day passes on

You cannot save time
  Use it wisely
    as you live
  You cannot hoard it
It is only here to give

You cannot save time
  in a cookie jar
    or a sack
  Once it's gone, it's gone
and you'll never get it back

You cannot save time
  It is so precious
    and rare
  But you can spend some with me
if you have the time to spare

UGANDA

The pearl of Africa has rotted away
  as hundreds of thousands have died
in a waste of innocent human life
  that is known as genocide

Soldiers of madmen have ravaged the land
  shot its sons and raped its daughters
Bones and skulls lay in its fields
  and blood flows in its waters

Madmen like Obote and Idi Amin
  leading carnivals of death and bloodshed
A circus of torture, rape, and pillage
  that leaves their own lying dead

And, if genocide is not enough abuse
  disease makes life even worse
The Aids virus now sweeps over the land
  'Slim' is what they call this curse

You may die running from a soldier's gun
  or you may die making love
You may be tortured in a hotel room
  and thrown alive
    off the roof
      high above

You may feel fear flow through your veins
  as you run to save your life
and turn to see your daughter gunned down
  or a soldier
    crush the skull
      of your wife

And helplessly you hide out in a field
  feeling pain far beyond all sorrow
Wondering how long you will survive
  or if the people will have a tomorrow

And here I sit
  in peace and silence
    in a land of democracy
sickened to learn
  of places on Earth
    where life's an atrocity

EASTER IN MUIR WOODS

Even within the comforts of peace
someone finds something
to fight about
And among the ruins
of waste and war
the poet finds beauty
to write about

TREASURES OF NATURE
(To Russ Scott)

Have you ever seen the Northern Lights?
Reaching
Jumping
Shivering
Illuminating the darkness
Fingers of light
springing up from the horizon
Curtains of satin
fluttering in the night
Now blue
Now green
Now white

Have you ever spent a night in the wilds?
Tranquillity
Solitude
Silence
Whispering winds
Far from artificial lights
and the drone of the city
Black still evenings
Crickets chirping
Fire flies
Falling stars
Unseen sounds

Have you ever felt starshadow?
　Subtle
　　Gentle
　　　Mellow
　　Soft as down
　Smooth as silk
A hush of light from the heavens
　Beyond beyond
　　and beyond imagination
　It settles
Touching you
　Touching me

Have you ever seen the moon set on the horizon?
　Slowly
　　Falling
　　　Glowing
　　Gradual transformation
　from silvery blue
to the deepest of red-orange
　Slowly diminishing
　　Falling gracefully
　Glowing like dawn
in the dark
　of midnight

I have seen the Northern Lights
I have spent many nights in the wilds
I have felt starshadow
I have seen
　the moon set
　　on the horizon
　and though they brought
not fame or fortune
　they made life rich
　　and full for me
　　　These treasures
　　　　of Nature

WITH A CUP OF TEA
(To Jacob and Latitia Shiner)

Here I sit with a cup of tea
thinking about writing some poetry
On a wet winter evening such as this
it's the next best thing to a soft, warm kiss

The dishes were washed and stacked and dried
picked up carefully, and put back inside
the cupboards where they all came down from
to serve me dinner when the cooking was done
Tonight, I had waffles with honey and butter
and the type of wine that flows from a cow's udder
I sprinkled a bit of cinnamon, just on top
of the waffles, that is, and I didn't want to stop
because eating them was so delicious and fun
but I felt warm and wonderful when they were done
They were crisp and hot and golden brown
with lots of thick honey dripping down
their sides and dropping onto to the plate
Now, how many were there that I ate?
At first, it was two and then it was four
and then I wanted to eat some more
But I stopped right there, not another did I eat
or I wouldn't fit into my pants next week!

Then, I sat back in my rocking chair
with a cup of hot tea beside me there
and thought of two little ones for whom I care
and of how I would like to share
a poem with little Jake and Tish
and share with them a little New Year's wish

May your year be filled with giggles and joy
May you always be a good little girl and boy
Always brush your teeth and wash your hands
and try very hard to understand
the things Mom and Daddy try to teach you
and why green is green and blue is blue
Why up is up and never down
Why a square is a square and never round
Why in is in and out is out
(and just what is this world all about?)
Why left is left and right is right
Why day is bright and dark is night

Why do I giggle when I'm pushed on a swing?
And what is it that makes me want to sing?
And why do I get those looks from Dad
when he thinks I'm being naughty and bad?
Doesn't he know that I'm trying to see
just how much he'll put up with from me?
And you know I do it to Mommy too
But, shhhh...that's just between me and you
I've been around and I know their style
and I know how much I can get with a smile
To me, candy and kisses are my kind of loot
and I know what I can get by just being cute
Though I may not know what this world's all about
I've got that much figured out!

METROMORPHOSIS

And more of the Bay is hidden away
　　by another tall building being raised
The natural skyline of hills is transformed
　　into straight lines
　　　　jagged and crazed

Down in a grid that is known as 'Downtown'
　　streets are shadowed for most of the day
Sunshine touches concrete for a moment at noon
　　but has a meeting
　　　　and must hurry away

It crawls up the building on the other side
　　and quickly disappears o'er the roof
and until high noon of the following day
　　it continues
　　　　to remain aloof

And down those corridors that the shadows own
　　the wind pushes and heaves in great gusts
Shoving like a woman at a one-day sale
　　Kicking up stray papers
　　　　and dust

Wrapping Wall Street Journals around walkers legs
  Leaving hair tossed and frayed in disarray
Then, taking a left at Montgomery and Pine
  blows its way
      away from the Bay

And generations ago, the settlers all came
  for the beauty or the riches of the soil
They saw that rewards were there to be won
  through patience
    with time
      and with toil

For miles they saw hills
  of sand and grass
that the future slowly smothered
  under brick and glass
And crowds continued to come
  to this city-by-the-shore
'til, alas!
  you can't see
    what they once came here for!

YOU'RE THE KIND OF GIRL I WANT

You're the kind of girl I want
  when all of my travels are through
If I didn't have these dreams in my head
  I'd have my arms wrapped around you
Though sometimes I feel like my life is a lie
  there's one thing that I know is true
You're the kind of girl I want
  when all of my travels are through

There are so many miles I've yet to run
and so many things I've yet to get done
  So many things I think I'm doing right
I know these feelings can tear me apart
when I reach inside my lonely heart
  and know you wouldn't mind
    being here with me tonight

I don't know why
　I think of my art as a saviour
I don't know why
　I think of you as an anchor
It could very well be
　that I am completely wrong

It could very well be
　that I'll run aground
on an uncharted sea
　with no one around
when I could have your love
　deep in my heart
　　beating strong

I'm sure your love
　could be my saving grace
if this were only
　another time and place
And to try to explain things
　would only make matters worse

One day, when I'm a memory
　that's faded to mist
your beautiful eyes
　may fall upon this
and you may make some sense
　of these reasons
　　written in verse

And, no matter if my life is all a lie
　or a sky full of dreams coming true
you're the kind of girl I want
　when all of my travels are through

STRESS

Tension, pressure
  frustration
A pace that makes you
  want to scream!
Sometimes, it seems
  like a nightmare
and so distant
  from a dream

In a moment
  I'd walk out and leave it
if I only could
  But tonight
with a cup of tea and a book
  I'll be feeling
    as I should

STRANGERS

Johnson, DeLong
  Atherton
    Miller, and Jones
  All strangers
from a strange land
  sent to take life
    from strangers
      in a strange land
Soldiers
  sitting in a field
    far away
  from anything they knew

The clean, blue sky
  Perfect, pure clouds
    Sensuous sunshine

They should be
  taking sweethearts to picnics
    in the park
      or countryside
They should be
  lying on the beach
    listening to the waves
      or thoughts in their minds
They should be
  washing and waxing
    their pride and joy
      waiting back home in a garage
They should be
  dancing or walking
    through city lights
  or hiking
in the solitude of tall forests

But they are here
  Strangers
    with rifles in their hands
  longing in their hearts
and letters from home
  Strangers
    from all corners and counties
  of their homeland
so far away
  Strangers
    hoping bullets will stray
  as long as this madness
and confusion prevails

Strangers
  unto themselves
    So young
      So much to explore
    Not even sure
  of who they themselves are
let alone why

Confused
  Frustrated
    Disenchanted
      Alone

After long hours
  of fear and explosions
    they sat in silence
separated from the world
In a daze, Johnson murmured
  "What the hell are we doing here?"
    DeLong shot back
  "You're here for God and Country
Sweet Freedom and Liberty
  America's milk and honey!"
    Atherton laughed nervously and said
  "Christ, DeLong
you'll be a general someday
  We're fighting for oil
    and natural resources"
  Then Miller added
"Yeah, that and the profits from arms sales"
  They fell to silence
    Miller looked at Jones
    Jones stood
looked at them all and said
  "You're here
    because a handful of politicians
  in our country
and a handful of politicians
  in this country
    can't communicate"
      Strangers
        one and all

GHOSTS OF WAR

The ghosts of war
  never seem to go away
    They seem to resurface
    day after day
And sometimes I wonder
  (between you and me)
    if peace on this planet
    could ever be

LOS ANGELES

Los Angeles!?
  That isn't a city!
It's a disease spreading out
  in every direction!
And that Golden Thing
  is a golden thing
and is just the ocean's reflection
  as seen from high above
on Mulholland Drive
  How many years had it been?
Hmmm...just about five

Jasmine tea and memories
  A conversation with Ai-Yen
Chinese food and a car wash
  A horror movie with Glen
Lights that brought on applause
  Some that only got a clap
Finding my way from Santa Monica
  by my wits, without a map

Snow up in The Grapevine
  Sunshine in Malibu
Fireworks in West L. A.
  A skyline completely in view
Wagner overtures at Big Rock
  Poetry and hot oatmeal
Words with Terri in Deustchland
  'How ya doin'?' and 'How do you feel?'

Talking about the old friends
  that are no longer around
And I see that some old haunts
  are now just holes in the ground
LaCienega and Sunset
  Ivar and Cherokee
Hollywood and Vine
  Melrose and North Whitley
Franklin and LaBrea
  Take a right when you get there
For Pete's sake! It's a disease!
  Spreading out everywhere!

FIND WHAT YOU CAN DO

When should I start to change my life?
  And where do I begin?
Just with a thought, a moment's pause
  of wondering where you have been

You may think you haven't the money to change
  But, is money what you first need?
I think it is knowledge
  and I wish that more people
consumed it with as much greed

But before all that knowledge comes interest
  You always need that to begin it
Nothing you learn will really stay with you
  unless you are interested in it

 So, find what you can do
  and do what you can do
  as well as you can do it
 And you'll find that life
  is an interesting thing
         as you live
   and find you're way
        through it

ALMOSTS, MAYBES, AND NEAR MISSES

It's not coming across
  the way it was intended
It's not the way it was supposed to be

There are feelings I am feeling
  that may never be mended
and you've created a different image of me

What I meant to say
  is not what you heard
The spirit changed as sound sailed
  through the air

And it's amazing and sad
  how one ill-timed word
can steal away all the chances
  that were there

So, all imagery and fantasy
  is now sour and dated
Excitement's disappointment and regret

And any greeting now
  would only seem belated
as our future is a past we can forget

ANOTHER EXCUSE

I've not felt like writing anything
  No ideas have come to mind
I hope I haven't lost interest
  Has ambition been left far behind?

My fingers are sore from work done today
  Where else can I find an excuse?
Perhaps, I could say that my pen's run dry
  (there's a hundred in the house I could use)

I don't know
  maybe I could say
    I've been feeling uninspired
That I have too many things to do
  or maybe I'm just feeling tired

Or maybe I just don't have the time
  Or maybe my mood is all wrong
I'll join you in hoping
  I come up with something
    worth reading before too long

THERE'S A FULL MOON GLOWING

There's a full moon glowing
   out my window tonight
as I sit here wishing
   I was holding you tight
Feeling your hug
   and your soft, warm kiss
But your hugs and kisses
   aren't all that I miss
I miss your voice
   your whispers, your sighs
I miss looking deep
   into your dark eyes
There's a full moon glowing
   and I guess that will do
as I hope you're missing me
   the way I'm missing you

FLICKERING FLAMES
(To John Savoy)

I wish I were in the woods right now
   sitting by a crackling fire
watching the tiny sparks fly up
   fading out as they zig-zag higher

There's something about staring at those flames
   in the darkness of the night
that soothes and puts a mind at ease
   and leaves labors feeling light

The smell of the smoke as it curls up
   in wisps and floats away
An aroma that says: " Your chores are done
   Now enjoy the rest of the day "

Sit back and run over some thoughts you have
   of days gone by or to come
And if you don't have any plans to think out
   sit back and dream up some

Throw another branch on the fading fire
  Gaze into the glowing coals
A fire, just as this one here
  has been shared by how many souls?

Oh, just about as far as time stretches back
  As far as imagination reaches
How many sat around one in primative caves
  or on ancient Persian beaches?

How many shepherds sat about one in a field
  watching their flocks fall to sleep?
How many an explorer built a fire on the trail
  or on the side of a mountain steep?

How many a cowboy built a fire in the gloaming
  to give rest to him and his horse?
To cook up some beans or maybe a rabbit
  and boil up some coffee, of course

How many a pirate built a fire on the shore
  after burying their stolen treasure?
And how many young lovers have built a fire
  to stare into for hours of pleasure?

How many an Indian built theirs in a tee-pee
  under wide prairie skies of blue?
And how many an Eskimo has built a fire
  in the middle of their domed igloo?

Ah, the magic of a fire is a mystery
  and I don't know if it's ever been clear
just why those flames and that crackling sound
  have drawn so many near

How many souls have sat around a fire?
  Perhaps one for each star in the sky
have sat watching flames dance to and fro
  with white smoke swirling up so high

Indeed, how many souls have sat around a fire
  How many, with or without names
have spent the better part of a long, dark night
  staring into those flickering flames?

PAPER CRANE
(TO MIHO KAWASHIGE)

In colors red
  and green and blue
Sent over the ocean
  to me, from you

So delicate and small
  So detailed and fragile
Folded by fingers
  so slender and agile

Forever in flight
  this crane will stay
Forever flying
  by night and day

And just where it goes
  nobody knows
    nor can I explain
The magical
  motionless flight
    of your paper crane

THE NECKTIE

My, my!
  Take off your tie
and see how attitudes change
I always thought
  that bit of cloth
dangling 'round my neck to be strange

If you wish to impress the masses
  you need not have a degree
Just put a tie around your neck
  and speak to them eloquently

Chances are, they'll listen to you
before they'll listen to me
That bit of cloth dangling from your neck
gives an air of authority

If you're seeking a higher position
superiors must be impressed
And they know you can't have
the brains of a wizard
unless you are properly dressed

If you have an idea or you're in a bind
and there's money to be raised
Wear a tie, say "God spoke to me!"
and your actions will surely be praised

If someone thinks: "Hmmm...what is this?
I wonder what this means?"
Will they seek the answer from a flannel shirt
and a pair of faded blue jeans?

Somehow, when a man puts on a tie
he thinks he's a cut above
and those who are in the abyss below
his attention, they're not worthy of

Some workingmen look at a guy with a tie
and think: "Here's a man I can't trust"
And some men with ties look back at him
with disdain or even disgust

I've lived on both sides, but don't believe me
Go and see, for your own sake
the difference a little bit of cloth
dangling from your shirt collar can make

SHANGHAIED
(To George W. Shiner)

Far out on the deep blue waters
  where the waves will swell as high
as a snow peaked mountain that pokes
  its head through clouds in the sky
Far from the smell of baked goods
  and the lonely seagull's cry
Far from the sweet, soft hush
  of a gentle young lover's sigh

A man slowly, painfully awakens
  and tries to lift his head
though it feels as if it's been weighted
  with a half ton of molten lead
He feels the ship's forecastle floor
  that served as last night's bed
and the rolling motion of the sea
  that fills his heart with dread

And the rolling motion whispered
  words not to be denied
Fear, anger, and anguish
  seized and froze him inside
And through his foggy thoughts
  he clearly realized
that, once again, without him knowing
  he had been shanghaied

As much as he tried in the past
  somehow he couldn't overcome
his need for smoke filled evenings
  and bottles of dark rum
And here again his drunkenness
  caused his life to come undone
by having another endless evening
  of rowdiness and fun

How many bottles were there?
  Two, three, or four?
Enough that he couldn't even recall
  his own Mum's name anymore
And how many years had those bottles
  led him time after time before

to waking up half dead and dazed
    on a ship's forecastle floor?

The months dragged by as they forged their way
    down to the merciless Horn
feeling ragged, rundown, and worthless
    wasted, weary, and worn
Overworked and underfed
    His clothes, tattered and torn
Wishing with every moment
    that he had never been born

And there below he was lost in dreams
    of sweet, soft lips, so lush
while above the wide, wooden decks were awash
    in snow, sleet, and slush
" ALL HANDS!!! " the first mate bellowed out
    and the crew scrambled forth with a rush
Commanded aloft with white-hot words
    that would make an old whore blush

And up into the ice-caked ropes
    they obeyed all of his commands
beating their fists against frozen canvas
    to keep feeling in their hands
Some would give their own right arms
    to smell the earthy smell of land
and some will certainly never again
    touch any shore of white sand

Now, down below, in water soaked clothes
    he watches a candle's wax drip
cocking his head to hear gusts of wind
    hoping another sail doesn't rip
And he swears to himself that he'll take the pittance
    that he'll be paid for this trip
and save for the future, a wife, and a farm
    and never again sail on a ship

But he knows he's only fooling himself
    It'll all be gone as before
the moment he catches a whiff of rum
    after he has set foot on shore
And if he's lucky he'll wake in the morn
    lying in the soft arms of a whore

and if he's not, he'll wake up in the scum
of a ship's forecastle floor

He knows he'll live and die as a sailor
as he knows he never was graced
with the looks, the money, or talent
to live a high life without haste
And his dreams of slipping his arms around
a young girl's slender, curved waist
will always be broken by a first mate screaming
" GET UP OR I'LL BEAT YOU TO PASTE!!! "

Such is the life of the sailor
To play, but never to win
To knock on opportunity's door
but never be allowed to walk in
To dream of a future, a wife, and a farm
while knowing it will be as it's been
Living the curse of a sailor's life
to be shanghaied
again and again

WHO'LL BUY MY DREAMS?

Who'll buy my dreams?
I'll sell them for a song
I've tried so hard
to find an ace in my cards
I've been losing too long

Who'll buy my dreams?
I've been watching them fade
It's hard to let go
of everything that you know
But, look at this mess I've made

I bet all I had
on stars and moonbeams
Who'll buy my dreams?

Who'll buy my dreams?
I'm left all alone
I went chasing the sun
Now, half of my lifetime's done
and I'm so far from home

Who'll buy my dreams?
I'll sell all or some
I'll sell them cheap
'cos I've been losing sleep
thinking of times to come

I bet all I had
on stars and moonbeams
Who'll buy my dreams?

Who'll buy my dreams?
Can I say I tried?
Why can't I be
like everyone else I see?
I can't be satisfied

Who'll buy my dreams?
I planned them so well
Maybe I'm not through
Maybe these dreams'll do
They say, "You never can tell"

I bet all I had
on stars and moonbeams
Who'll buy my dreams?

GRANDPA'S COLDEST WINTER

This must be the coldest winter
I can remember
It hasn't let up
since the first of November
Always snow or sleet or slush
covering the ground

And above has been a blanket
  as black as coal
    through which the sun hasn't been able
  to burn a hole
and, on this side
  not a ray of sunshine can be found

Oh! I can remember
  back in seventy-four
    in one night it snowed
  two feet or more
and the town lay peacefully still
  frosted in white

Knee deep, I walked on
  for many a mile
    just to see one of
  my true love's smiles
and I trudged back home again
  that very night

On school mornings
  there was hot chocolate in a cup
    before being buckled and buttoned
  and bundled up
until all you could see
  were two little smiling eyes

But there was enough of a cheek
  for a kiss from Mother
    and off you shuffled
  walking somehow or another
Little bundles of clothing
  moving under the gray dawn skies

And then there was the warmth
  when you first walked in
    of the welcome smells of dinner
  coming from the kitchen
The dog's wagging tail and warm licks
  to your cold, red face

Mom saying: "Be sure
  to knock off all the snow

Shut the door
You're letting all the heat out, you know?
And be sure all your boots and coats
are back in place"

There was snowman building
and snowball fights
Snow crunching under foot
on quiet walks at night
and Christmas lights
of so many colors glowing

But winter was never here
for certain
until, one day
somebody pulled back a curtain
and jumped up smiling and shouting:
"It's snowing! It's snowing!"

Oh, but winter can be
a cold and miserable thing
Making us wait
through long months until spring
when, finally, we can again
see bright, blue skies

And then it'll be
just a matter of time
when the summer months bring
to your mouth and mine
a wedge of Grandma's
freshly baked fruit pies

Now, what is this?
A Grandchild's voice I hear
telling me I say the same thing every year?
Well I...
why I...
yes, I must admit it's true

I do say it's the coldest winter
I can remember
when I'm sitting here
in the midst of December
wishing again
that the skies were bright and blue

SUNSHINE, BLUE SKY

Sunshine
  Blue sky
    Red maple trees

Snowflakes
  Dark clouds
    Breathtaking breeze

Moonbeams
  Dog days
    Starshadow's ease

Raindrops
  Springtime
    Wet to the knees
Puddles will tease
Splash around in them
  as much as you please
Soon wintertime
will cause them
to freeze

LIFE'S LITTLE TREASURES
(To Megan Belisle)

Old photographs
  Boxed memories
    Forgotten names
      of familiar faces
    Trinkets, postcards
  keepsakes, and mementos
Souvenirs from foreign places
  Dusty thoughts
    and nostalgic pleasures
  awakened by
life's little treasures

I like to laugh a lot
  Don't you?
It's especially good
  to find a laugh
when you're feeling blue
  Those times
when you're feeling down
  and don't know
what to do
  I like to laugh a lot
Don't you?

It's fun to share a laugh
  with a friend
The kind that brings tears
  to the eyes
and cause your knees to bend
  A laugh by phone
face to face
  or in a card
    you send
  It's fun to share a laugh
with a friend

I like to laugh a lot
  don't you?
Though there are times
  when we all
must cry a little too
  But if I were
to choose my mood
  I must say
this is true:
  I like to laugh a lot
Don't you?

WHO CAN YOU LOOK UP TO?

At some point in everyone's childhood
you cling to your heroes that represent good
Who, against all odds always seem to win
and you want to grow up to be just like them

The Batmans and Supermans and basketball stars
The fastest drivers of the fastest cars
The cowboy who always gets the bad guy
and gets hit now and then, but'll never cry

Heroes that influence with the good they teach
Who help you to dream, who help you to reach

The poets of old, the writers of song
The heroes who never do anything wrong
The composer of music, the author of a book
Those who give the future a polished look

But who are we to look up to anymore
when our leaders sell terrorists weapons of war
and call the men 'heroes' who performed the task?
Who can you look up to?
  This question I ask

Million dollar preachers fall one by one
who sneak off to hotels when the sermon is done
Who use tears to punctuate the purity they preach
but don't seem to practice the lessons they teach

And people complain
  about young people's goals
    That they don't think enough
      with their hearts and souls
All this may be certain
  a reality and true
    But who is there that they
      can all look up to?
In this fast-food world
  being built for speed
    where patience isn't listed
      as being a need?

Where people only seek
  instant gratification
    as the immediate answer
     to all situations?

Young people are able to form their own views
and what do they see on the evening news?
The top lawmaker breaking laws himself
and walking away, unlike everyone else
or if he does get punished for his illegal ways
  he'll get a harsh headline
    and ninety days

What kind of thoughts go through a young person's head
when they find out that drugs struck a hero dead?
Or when someone they thought could never fail
has just been found guilty and sentenced to jail?

Know now that life can be a long, hard road
but don't expect someone else to carry your load
Believe in your dreams
  Find your heroes and leaders
but don't fall for the frauds
  the liars
    and cheaters

DREAMS

I find it a wonderful
  and honorable thing
    to believe in the magic of dreams
    To see something as it could be
  and not only as it is
or seems

Where have all the explorers gone?
  And the brave, bold pioneers?
Have we lost our sense of adventure
  in these maddening, modern years?

Everyone sits back, playing it safe
  So afraid to take a chance
And love is almost amusing
  Whatever happened to romance?

Love letters are now a dying art
  Music almost has lost all its feeling
And something has happened to Christmas now
  that's so commercial and unappealing

Creativity and craftsmanship
  have somehow become old-fashioned
Where has common courtesy gone?
  Where are wisdom, kinship, and passion?

Quality itself has become exotic
  A rare commodity
It seems that self-esteem and pride
  are now mediocrity

Depth in art is less important now
  than glitter and sensation
And love scenes written nowadays
  leave little to imagination

Somewhere, it seems our civilization
  had a cultural collision
that took away family togetherness
  and left us the television

Live music at home was a common practice
  not very long ago
Now, if there's music in the home at all
  it's a tape deck or a radio

We began as a creature, intelligent enough
  to only live bare in the bush
Have we come all this way to have only the brains
  to learn which buttons to push?

We can now push buttons to keep us warm
   and feed us our daily bread
To shave our faces and underarms
   and to dry the hair on our heads

We can push buttons that turn darkness to light
   and push them to fly through the air
We can push them to turn on cartoon shows
   to keep the kids out of our hair

We can push them and talk to someone we know
   ten thousand miles away
We can talk to them in tomorrow
   as they talk to yesterday

We can talk to some old, long lost friend
   or say hello to our mother
We can push them for drinks and candy bars
   or push them to kill one another

Where have all the great composers gone?
   The great thinkers and great debators?
Where are the mathematicians
   now that calculus is calculators?

Perhaps, I'm being a bit too harsh
   But I'll leave a question to linger
Have we traded the strength of the human mind
   for the strength of the index finger?

THE NEW FRONTIER

There once was a time when you could hear
the courageous call of the pioneer
Who cried out in a voice, patriotic and clear
"We must move west to the new frontier!"

Thousands, the western horizon did lure
and gave them a fever only travel could cure
Some sold all but supplies, horse, and gun
to follow their hearts and the red setting sun

The fur trappers were first to wander inside
with their sense of survival their only guide
The deep wilderness was their destination
that quenched their thirst for isolation

Covered with buckskin from head to toe
Going places only an Indian would go
They lived in the wilds for most of their lives
Some taking Indians to be their wives

The thrill of adventure was wind in their sails
as they left behind them their westward trails
that became the pioneer's only means
to follow them west as they followed their dreams

With Canada to the north
  and to the south the Rio Grande
they saw limitless opportunities
  in this new wild land
And they came by the thousands
  through the Cumberland Gap
with the millions of stars
  as their only map

By horse and wagon they came
  moving towards the Great Plains
at the slow, crawling pace of a snail
Inching their way
  day by day
Blazing that new westward trail

With sheep, swine, and steers
  these bold pioneers
came to tame these unknown lands
To build a new world
  as history unfurled
with a will and the strength in their hands

Wrestling with the odds
  some built houses of sod
those who settled out there on the plains
And they all came to see
  that their new reality
would involve toil, courage, and pain

The wide, open spaces with rich, fertile soil
    were the stuff that their dreams were made of
Stretching out forever, as far and as wide
    as the expanse of light blue up above

There came the fur trader and the Texas rancher
    and there came a new breed of squatters
and as time passed by, Nature brought the frontier
    new little sons and daughters

But the restless white man
    was not alone on this land
This was also the Indian's home
The red man, it seems
    wasn't in his new dreams
and he wanted it all for his own

Then, both people's blood
    spilled forth in a flood
as white man called red man a savage
Some came only to farm
    Never meaning to harm
While others came only to ravage

During this conquest
    there was so little rest
for the red man or the white pioneer
Neither side would give
    as both sides lived
in a dark cloud of hatred and fear

History saw both sides pay a dear price
    as Nature saw both sides sacrifice
Now came a new rule that most understood
    and that rule was:
        Get, while the gettin's good!

Although, there was more than anyone could need
    the dreamy quality was lost to greed
Out here in the wilds
    with no laws to be breaking
anything and everything
    was theirs for the taking

Some moved farther, out and beyond to the west
as their pioneer fever would give them no rest
And out in California, up at Sutters Mill
came the cry: *There's gold in them there hills*!

While, in Texas, they drove their cattle north
'til the railroad's endless rail stretched forth
and brought an end to round-ups and cattle drives
as farms told the open range to step aside

From Atlantic to Pacific
  one land had been born
    From hard work, blood, and battle
      it was quickly formed
as they came to conquer Nature
  instead of befriending it
    Never bowing to it
      but twisting and bending it

And as the frontier faded, year after year
So did the adventurous pioneer
Day after day, the era retreated
  a time in history
    that will not be repeated

POLARIS

Polaris
  North star
    Bright star

How many souls
  have searched for you
    through treetops
  between clouds
in the wilderness
  seeking a clue?

Seeking some sense
  of direction in darkness
    Fur trappers
    Bounty hunters
  Nomads, explorers
    Sea captains too

How many souls
  have sighed at the sight
    of heavy skies
    breaking, glistening?
Bringing you back
  glowing, piercing through

Star of love
  Brightest of all
    First to arrive
  Last to leave
Saviour of the lost
  Shining true

    Bright star
  North star
Polaris

SNOWFLAKES ON SUTTONS BAY
(To George M. Shiner)

Like a fluid snow scene you've shaken up
  to see the snow swirling around
This is how the world looks today
  as snowflakes swirl to the ground

So lightly are they lifted and carried away
  So softly do they float on the breeze
So slowly do they make their way to the ground
  to land with such silent ease

Frosting the world in a blanket of white
  A blanket that moves and shifts
as winter winds whip their way through the woods
  to leave them piled high in soft drifts

As tenderly as notes of a piano sonata
  they sway and waltz through the air
Landing to bend the full branches of pine trees
  and highlight those autumn left bare

So peaceful do they leave the mood of the woods
  when a new storm is on the way
that will blacken the sky, bring chilling winds
  and leave snowflakes
    on Suttons Bay

HILLS OF LEELANAU

Oh, I can't forget what I saw
  in the hills of Leelanau
Oh, the beauty of it all
  All the beauty
    in the hills of Leelanau

Lake Michigan
  The deep blue of the bay
Oh, the views
  that leave nothing to say
And the fresh pine smell in the air
  follows me everywhere

Leaves in autumn
  and the touch of velvet wind
makes me feel
  like I'm back home again
And a sunset
  as you walk down the beach
makes you feel like all your dreams
  are in your reach

Oh, I can't forget what I saw
  In the hills of Leelanau
Oh, the beauty of it all
  All the beauty
    in the hills of Leelanau

A SIMPLE MAN LIKE ME

An ice cream and a long walk
under what few stars I see
These simple pleasures satisfy
A simple man like me

A good book and some music
and hot peppermint tea
make a pleasant, well spent evening
for a simple man like me

A cabin in the country
A good wife and family
These warm things would surely please
a simple man like me

A cabin, wife, and family
my music and poetry
These things fill the many dreams
of a simple man like me

I need not gold nor silver
diamonds or jewelery
to satisfy the daily needs
of a simple man like me

I need to walk tall forests
and to hear a roaring sea
These things always seem to please
a simple man like me

A plate of good food
A glass of fine wine
An evening with good company
is enough to please and occupy
a simple man like me

To work a little more each day
at what I strive to be
This is the daily goal
of a simple man
like me

COFFEE BREAK

A cup of coffee
  Kick up your feet
    Relax
      and take a pause
    Rest a few moments
  before you continue
working for your cause

WHERE DOES THE WIND GO?

He pours another glass of wine
and continues to spin a yarn
about the old days
when bums were called hobos
'Hobo' has a romantic sound to it
but bums is just bums

Hobos sat around small fires
waiting for the whistle of a train
while cooking something in a tin can
Waiting for the wind
and the Southern Pacific
to carry him somewhere
Anywhere
No hurry
No appointments to keep
No bills to pay

Where does the wind go?
  Ask a hobo
    He'll know
He's chased that wind
like a youngster chases bubbles
Like a young man chases girls
Like a poet chases dreams
Like a dog chases rabbits
Like the sun'll chase the moon

He's chased it
east to west
north to south
and back again
Been beaten
and befriended
battered
and broken

He don't laugh much...
except at the world
and all the suckers
that pay to ride trains
and all the suckers
that bury themselves deeper
and deeper
into debt
and situations that keep them
bound and gagged
restricted and restrained
so far and no further
Anchored to life
with only one alteration
A once-a-year
free-for-all
visit-the-relatives
vacation

But a hobo has no relatives
except coyotes, maybe
or stray dogs
or a full moon
He can count the stars
He can kill time
like it's nobody's business

And, I suppose
if anyone knows
where the wind goes
when it drifts and blows
it's the hobos

Where does the wind go?

I'M NOT FEELING RIGHT TONIGHT

I'm not feeling right tonight
I don't feel like eating a bite tonight
Inspiration is not in flight tonight
My visions are not in sight tonight
I'll stay in bed curled up tight tonight
This fever was more than slight tonight
And I have nothing to write tonight
  No, not a thing right
    to write tonight

SEASON TICKET

Down the stairs I climb
  to find my seat
    I settle in to relax
Before me, an ocean of empty seats
  will soon be
    an ocean of backs

High up here
  in the second tier
    where crescendos swell
      and each note rings clear
High up here
  above it all
    in a San Francisco
      symphony hall

Lost in the rows
  of empty, black chairs
are three lone figures
  keeping busy down there
And, though tonight's program
  is not to start soon
they have come out to practice
  and to get in tune

One on flute
  One on harp
    One behind the xylophone
These three fiddle about
  on the stage
    all alone

And now the lonely trio
  becomes a full quartet
as a bassist stands on stage
  who hasn't found his seat, just yet
And the big bass leans against him
  like a drunken, long lost friend
who puts his arm around you and says
  'Have you gotta dollar to lend?'
He finds his seat
  sits down
    tightens his bow
      and smoothes his coat
then allows his big bass fiddle
  to groan out its first deep note

Cascades of wonder come trailing forth
  from the harp of many strings
It is always a peaceful and soothing song
  this beautiful instrument sings
of waterfalls or raindrops
  or babbling brooks flowing
Cool shade under a willow tree
  with dabs of summer sun showing

A trio of basses
  now play on their own
    with sounds, both moving and mellow
and are joined by a lone violin
  an oboe, a clarinet
    and a duo of cellos

One by one
  the musicians all trickle in
    in tuxedo or long, flowing gown
One by one
  the audience, too, trickles in
    for a musical night on the town

The audience itself
begins to tune up
Chatting, laughing, and flipping pages
They've come to visit
with one another
and hear the music of the ages

A trumpet blares out
a regal passage
Noble and daring, of course
The crescendo continues to climb
as the orchestra
reaches full force

Audience and orchestra
compete and converse
both sounding
nearly the same
Tuba, trombone
viola, french horn
long bells
in a large silver frame

The double doors close
The house lights dim
Applause explodes in a burst
The conductor comes out
takes a sweeping bow
and begins to direct the first
concerto
sonata
tone poem
or symphony
Any of these
will certainly please

And when the piece closes
with triumphant climax
the musicians can pause
sit back
and relax
as applause
swells and roars
thundering off the walls

and in waves
swells again
for each curtain call

And again
dear ol' orchestra
you gave me good reason
to again
purchase tickets
to the upcoming season

ATTRACTION AND HESITATION

You don't have to read between the lines
to know how I feel for you
And I need not ask a single question
to know you feel the same too

Your eyes say you wish to bring down the silence
that stands between us like a wall
and all that would take is a simple greeting
a single word, that's all

But, somehow, we let it all linger there
to hang in time and wait
Both of us wish we had met yesterday
but, still we hesitate

How foolish can the two of us be?
It would only take one word
You could ask my name, I already know yours
One day, I overheard

The lingering is a bit exciting
We can guess the where and when
And if we don't meet
I have felt this before
and I guess I will feel it again

I SHOWED MY LOVE MY LOVE

I gave my love a ring
  but she threw the ring away
I gave my love a lovebird
  but she said it couldn't stay
I gave my love a locket
  that she never ever wore
I showed my love my love
  but she showed me the door

I gave my love a flower
  but she let it wilt and die
I gave my love a smile
  but she simply passed me by
I told my love I loved her
  as I had never loved before
I showed my love my love
  but she showed me the door

Ah! A fool in love
  to the truth is blind
    and will only see
      what he sees in his mind

He believes in tomorrow
  and the changes it'll bring
    and can't believe love
      could be a devious thing

I gave my love my heart
  but she broke it right in two
I gave my love my soul
  but she said it wouldn't do
I gave my love my life
  and wished that I could give her more
I showed my love my love
  but she showed me the door

And the love I gave
  was like a river
    flowing to the sea
It flowed in one direction
  and never came back
    to me

Some are folks
  who ran clean out of luck
  and some ran away from home
Some are folks
  thrown out on the streets
  to travel through life all alone

Curling up in a doorway somewhere
  to try to sleep out of the rain
But it's hard to hide from a howling wind
  from the snow
    or the cold
      or the rain

The pain of having no hopes, no dreams
  no faith in the next passing minute
Knowing that there is a world around them
  while having no certain place in it

And then there are those
  who have just given up
    who live that way by choice
Who have no ambition
  no place in this world
    Who don't care to have a voice

I've seen those who live day by day, somehow
  finding their food in the trash
I've seen people reach out their hands to them
  I've seen them refuse offered cash

Though they wander aimlessly and never smile
  someway, somehow this is their lifestyle
A style I don't pretend to understand

Those who are at the very bottom of the pile
  Who haven't known love for such a long, long while
    but won't accept
      an outreached helping hand

I'm so tired of the aimless way
  life has been treating me
I've been pushed and prodded down a path
  I thought I'd never see
But I haven't stopped doing what I wish
  with the time that I have on my hands
and I'm longing for my feet to walk
  upon the whispering sands

Far from this brittle landscape
  spreading out like a dreaded disease
I want to sit and watch the clouds
  as I embrace a breeze
But, here I am in a place so thick
  I can hardly make my way through it
I am just another tooth in a gear
  who is only adding to it

And I wonder what really keeps a person
  bound to such a place
when they could be drawing drafts of air
  pine scented and laced with a trace
of wild flowers and cherry blossoms
  or the saltiness of the seas
Allowing their troubles to fall away
  with such unchallenged ease

I long to pull my shirt over my head
  and feel the sun on my skin
instead of being here, chained behind a desk
  and spending my days locked in
an office where I only see the sun
  shining outside of tall, wide windows
I long to be where the hawk flies free
  and where the wild wind blows

Long ago, I took my handsome watch
  and threw it in back of a drawer
And all I wish to see rushing
  are waves as they rush to the shore
I no longer wish to hear sirens howl
  engines moan, or tires screech
Give me a silent sunset's glow
  with gulls gliding over the beach

Some people can't leave the city's drone
But I would not think it strange
for one to wish for the chance to sit
and watch the seasons change
I've heard the moan and groan and drone
I've obeyed and been bent by demands
Now I only wish to hear the waves
as I walk upon whispering sands

TO WATCH LIFE DISAPPEAR

Ah! There is so much to do
So much to read and write
There are never enough hours
in a day
Never enough in a night

Even with my best intentions
Even if I awaken at dawn
it seems the day takes a few steps
turns around
and is already gone

But if I can get just one thing done
for every day of the year
I will not be one
who waits around
to watch life
disappear

THE LAND DEVELOPER

I stand alone, deep in the woods
  entranced and enthralled
where a land developer would stand
  and probably guffaw, appalled:

"Why, look around and about you
  It's absolutely clear
that a brand new hamburger stand
  should be built right here
Tear up these shrubs and ferns
  and get rid of that blasted stream
You can bet your bottom dollar
  this is a shareholder's dream!"

"Build a little park
  to keep the kids out of Mom's hair
Mow down that grassy meadow
  and put a golf course there
with a country club behind it
  and condos to the right
Ah! By God!
  Won't it be a glorious sight?"

"Be rid of this dark forest
  Its varmints and its critters
and put up a little bakery
  to sell hot apple fritters
A few soft-hearted fools will say
  'The forest should stay there'
But rip it up
  Send me the bill
    I won't be here
      So, why should I care?"

LIFE

You come in
  and go out alone
    and in between face
      or fear the unknown

DON'T TAKE ANY WOODEN TICKLES
(To Jacob Shiner)

You can go and take a long walk in the sun
You can pull a girl's hair, if it's just for fun
You can color all the pictures in a coloring book
You can climb up a tree to take a look
You can wear all kinds of hats on your head
You can slide down a snow covered hill on a sled
You can say your ABC's and count to ten
and then start saying them over again
You can sing about birds and flowers and trees
You can sing about anything that you please
You can skip down a road or skip a rope
or make big bubbles with bubble soap
You can eat a cookie or chew on some gum
as long as you save little sister some
You can ride your wagon or fly a plane
or splash in puddles walking in the rain
You can make funny faces and make new friends
or show Dad how to wash the car on weekends
You can throw a penny to make a wish
You can eat everything that's put on your dish
You can look at pictures from all kinds of places
You can learn how to tie your own shoe laces
You can wash your hands real good for Momma
You can learn to use a period and a comma
You can learn to name all fifty states
to be quiet when you should and not stay up late
You can eat ice cream and cake
    or hot dogs and pickles
        but listen...
        don't take any wooden tickles!

I SEWED A PATCH UPON MY JEANS
(To Keith Shiner)

I sewed a patch upon my jeans
    because it's never bothered me
        to have a patch upon my knee
    for the whole world
to look at and see

And if there's a hole
  in the seat of my pants
    I'll sew another patch there
  It really doesn't matter to me
if the whole world stops to stare

Some people act
  like a hole in their pants
    feels the same as a hole in their leg
And that if they dare
  put a patch over it
    they must put out their hand and beg

Ah! The ego is such a delicate thing
  and pride shan't take a chance
to ever be seen in public
  with a little cloth patch
    on their pants

My goodness!
  What would the neighbors think?
    What would little, old ladies say
if I continue to wear
  patches on my pants
    'stead of throwing them away?

WEDNESDAY ORANGES AGGRESSIVELY PANCAKES

Wednesday oranges aggressively pancakes
  Is that what I said?
July apricots quietly typewriter
  I meant, "Hi. How are you?" instead

Baroque honeydew attentively harpsichord
  Life is a state of mind
Space-age artichoke lovingly blue shoes
  But don't be left behind

Century watermelon dynamically rain hat
  Theatre of the comically tragic
Saturday mango passively tango
  Interest plus practice is magic

October banana understandably spark plug
  You are what you consume
Precambrian persimmon indubitably oyster
  But there's only so much room

Romantic apple unquestionably flashlight
  Dreams are simple and breezy
Medieval strawberry relentlessly soap suds
  But realize nothing is easy

Future cranberry unknowingly log cabin
  Life is here to explore
Tomorrow tomato tenderly tire iron
  but don't hide behind the door

ONLY TOMORROW KNOWS

I think of you
  as I'm sitting here
    with this glass of wine
Wondering if the day will come
  when I'll think of you
    as mine

And I think about
  your sweet, full lips
    Your dark brown eyes that shine
and I wonder if
  our lips will touch
    If those eyes will look into mine

Will I feel your hand
  slip into mine?
    Will I let my feelings show?
Will you wrap your arms
  around me tightly?
    Only tomorrow knows

THERE'S SOMETHING OUT THERE

I'd like to get out on the highway again
and feel the wind rush in the window
Get out and visit a thousand towns
Nowhere where I have been, though

With nothing but adventure in the road ahead
Leaving mile after mile behind me
Without a phone or an address
It would be mighty hard to find me

Always wondering what tomorrow may bring
with not a worry in the world of today
Taking it all just as it comes
with no obligations in the way

The wonder of feeling how big this world is
as you wander through towns and new places
And the strangeness of going weeks at a time
seeing no familiar faces

Finding yourself at the edge of one state
as the sunrise finds a new day
And having another state under your wheels
as twilight is fading away

Driving through the dark
gazing at the bright stars
thinking over your situation
Paying no attention
to the growing static
of a fading radio station

Then you reach down to fumble
at the knobs without looking
at the soft glow of the radio
And you spin that dial
'til you find a country station
playing Sweethearts Of The Rodeo

They'd be singing Hey Doll Baby
with those satin voices
in sweet two-part harmony

that'll make you dance
   put chills up your spine
   and make you wish
      you were in Tennessee

And, just for fun, you start singing along
and howling at a full moon
as a rumbling feeling way down inside
says you better find a cafe soon

And you find yourself a little roadside joint
   with a sign that says: "WE NEVER CLOSE"
Time to take a break, have a piece of pie
   and keep yourself from taking a doze

And that's a welcome sound
   you hear under your wheels
      as you pull in the loose gravel lot
You can already taste
   that blueberry pie
      and feel your hands 'round a mug
         steaming hot

You walk up to the place
   smoothing back your hair
      and feel the coolness of the night
You hear a little music
   from the jukebox inside
      and some june bugs
         buzzin' 'round the lights

A sweet, little waitress says:
   "Thar ya be"
      as she takes a cup o' coffee
         from a tray
You say: "Honey,
   where'd you get that accent from?"
      She says: "Right here,
         in Albion, P-A"

You throw down your tip and pay your tab
   It's time to get back on the road
There ain't nothin'
   like takin' a break with a coffee
      and a piece of fresh pie
         ala mode

You stick a mint toothpick
   in between your teeth
      and give the key a quick turn
Looking down at the gauges
   you can see that you've
      got a few more miles to burn

And then it's on to Cheyenne
   Chicago
      Miami
         Montgomery
            Detroit
               and Boston
                  The Big Apple
                  Philly
               and Bangor, Maine
            Columbus
         Topeka
and Austin

San Francisco, Seattle
   Baltimore, Atlanta
      and all points in between
The way I feel right now
   I don't want to stop
      'til there ain't a place
         I haven't seen

There's always been something
   a little crazy about me
      that won't let me settle down
That's not satisfied
   unless I'm on a ride
      that takes me from town to town

And it's not that I'm
   of a reckless sort
      And it's not that I don't care
There's just always been a voice
   inside my head
      saying: "Hey, boy,
         there's something out there!"

CREEPY
(To Glen G. Gowen)

There's a strange creepy feeling
  crawling up my back
    like something is watching me
And there's a cat outside
  screeching at the moon
    peeking through the limbs of a tree

Every noise I hear makes me jerk and jump
  I hold my breath to listen real hard
I swear I heard something scurry around outside
  in the darkness of the backyard

I know there's someone waiting in my closet
  or they may be hiding in the shower
Yes, hiding behind the curtain and waiting
  to come out in the midnight hour

And I dare not try to sit back in my chair
  Someone may put a knife to my throat
or bash my head in with a baseball bat
  and steal away in a blood-stained raincoat

My flesh tingles and crawls
  with every sound I hear
    Every creak I hear the house make
As I sit here alone
  all by myself waiting
    for the dawn
      or my nerves
        to break

BOREDOM

You cannot blame
  anyone but you
    when you can't find
  anything to do

STRIKE UP THE BAND

I took a drive downtown tonight
  to hear music that I like
only to find that the orchestra
  had decided to go on strike

And I thought to myself
  How strange this is
    and why should they complain?
They're far from being beggars
  panhandling for change in the rain

They're not stuck behind a desk all day
  or operating machines
that bang and clatter and clunk all day
  leaving you all but clean

Somehow, I don't quite understand
  how they think they've got it so bad
If I could play music as my career
  I would be pretty damn glad

But musicians want more everyday
  and the workingman wants even more
While it always seems the poor teacher
  stands on the wrong side of the door

There is only so much in this world
  and the unions want it all
But somehow I think it's safe to say
  that they'll cause themselves to fall

A thousand times
   I have sat down to write
      a letter to a long, lost friend
Just a few words
   to stay in touch
      Just a simple greeting to send

I place the pen down
   upon the page
      and write "Dear..." so and so
and then it seems
   I have nothing to say
      It was all so long ago

For a moment it seems
   like a century's passed
      Like a different time or place
And I wonder...
   if it would be awkward for us
      if we met up face to face

But, then again
   we may talk on and on
      and not run out of things to say
We may talk on about
   what we're doing now
      or of memories of yesterday

You may think
   that I don't care anymore
      But you should know that's not true
And I'm glad I had the chance
   to meet up with someone
      as unforgettable
         and unforgotten
            as you

A TRILOGY OF TWISTED SATURDAY NIGHTS

A trilogy
  of twisted saturday nights
lay in the bottom of a gorge
Once rubber
  from the rubber tree
Once metal from the forge

Once rolling
  from the assembly lines
in brilliant blue and radiant red
Once rolling
  down the highway
now lay still, crumpled and dead

Was it dark
  in Topanga Canyon
on those fateful saturday nights?
Was it raining?
  Was the wind blowing hard?
Were they driving without their lights?

Was one
  a weary traveller
working late at the office one night
who dozed off
  as the winding road
twisted to the right?

Was one
  a drunken lover
driving to forget a fight
with his lover
  (who didn't literally mean
that this was his last night!)?

Was one
  some crazy person
trying to roar off into flight?
If he thought his car
  was lighter than air
I'm afraid he wasn't right

A trilogy
  of twisted saturday nights
now lay rusting by a creek
I crawled down
  one friday morning
just to take a peek

ANOTHER SUNDAY MORNING
(At Caffe Zephyr)

I've had one cup of coffee
  and I'm working on number two
as I spend a weekend morning
  the way that I usually do

With a great big bran muffin
  served warm with butter and jam
I scribble down words in my journal
  in the search for who I am

Leonardo's blue sky
  has no clouds today
    as the world moves along far below
    One side of which
  is sound to sleep
while the other is on the go

My brother dropped by, unexpectedly
  We sat and had a talk
He's gone home to work on a project
  I've come here to go for a walk

And here on the edge of a continent
  I see sailboats
    dot the bay

I'll sit on a log
  collect some thoughts
    and then I'll be on my way

NOT ENOUGH

A pot of homemade soup
  slowly simmers on the stove
    as the sky softly fades from blue to gray

The Sun Goddess swallows
  the glowing sun once more
    before giving birth to another day

And, in the silence of my room
  I only hear the soup boil
    I only see all the things I need to do

I only touch all my dreams
  that seem to be real
    Just out of reach, but clearly in my view

What did I do today
  to bring tomorrow to me?
    What did I do to draw the future near?

'Not enough'
  an inner voice whispers to me
'Not enough'
  it always whispers in my ear

I am a slave to my art
  and I never do enough
    to keep it or myself satisfied

And when that inner voice whispers:
  'Not enough, not enough'
    it was a day
      I can't say
        that I tried

GLORIFIED GREED

Where can you find orange juice
  that tastes like orange juice anymore?
Where can you find a house that's built
  as they were built before?
Try to find a tomato
  that tastes like one in a store
Have we traded away quality
  for the right to ask for more?

Card companies and Congress
  made each day a holiday
The evening news continues to have
  little of value to say
A few sick minds have taken the fun
  of Halloween away
Somewhere we lost some ethics
  that we had yesterday

Television preachers
  became manipulating crooks
Young people no longer care
  to learn anything from books
While television teaches
  brains are less important than looks
And microwave technique
  is today's version of someone who cooks

Somewhere along the line
  we've become a curious breed
that set aside care and quality
  for mass production and speed
We allow fashion and media
  to dictate wants and needs
And replaced our virtues and values
  with a villain called glorified greed

THE THIRD WAVE
(To Alvin Toffler)

The third wave is upon us
  Where can you hide from change
that creeps up and consumes you
  or leaves you feeling strange?

The only way to run from change
  is to run blind in the dark
fearing the light in the distance
  as you fear a mad dog's bark

The longer you hold yourself from it
  the farther you fall behind
Reach into your soul
  open it up
    seek out
      and you will find

Change will cease
  when white-capped waves
    refuse to reach the shore
You'll never live
  to know it all
    and there will always be more

The third wave is upon us
  and Earth cries out
    with urgency
for us to commit ourselves to change
  before we create
    an emergency

PROCRASTINATION

I have so many things that I want to do
  Their weight sometimes brings me sorrow
when I think of all I could have done today
  that I have put off 'til tomorrow

THE SUMMIT

An obsession with possession
A need for greed
Blinded by trends and fashion

No demand to understand
or yearn to learn
Not in touch with feeling or passion

So convinced they're standing
at the summit
when they couldn't be
any farther from it

WEDNESDAY

Wednesday
is a good day of the week
Everything
has just about reached its peak

Thursday
you're in the home stretch
You almost feel alive
And it all starts making sense
on friday
around five

DESPITE ALL OF THE ARGUMENTS

Despite all of the arguments:
If there are no creatures around
and a tree drops in the wilderness
I still say
there's going to be sound

JUST AS I PLEASE

If I were to do just as I please
perhaps, I'd sail off to the seas
and be a sailor; bold, bright, and brave
who'd challenge tempest and towering wave
Who'd fear not the northeaster's mighty blow
and stand in awe of the northern light's glow
Who'd climb the ropes and booms and spars
and walk his watch under millions of stars
that reach to horizons in all directions
and appear on the sea as rippling reflections
Tiny little lights glistening so high above
chosen by lovers in a moment of love
to be a symbol of fidelity year after year
Ah! But all of that is but fantasy out here!
Out here it is but ship and sea and man
wind, water, waves, and wild weather far from land
Rocking to and fro atop the mighty deep
rattled out of a much needed slumbering sleep
to climb the ropes at midnight in a hard driving sleet
to raise or lower a frozen canvas sheet
that serves as a sail to capture the wind
to take us far away from where we have been
and to wild wonders we wish to travel to
If I could do as I please, that's what I might do

If I were to do just as I choose
perhaps, I'd put on some wandering shoes
to wander through valleys and hills and dales
through sunshine and thunder and snow and gales
To hike up mountains, majestic and steep
lie down under stars and fall to sleep
and dream of what my tomorrow may bring
A vine covered cave or a clear hidden spring
with waters as sweet as wild honey and wine
as clear as crystal in the bright sunshine
To wander away to where I've never been
one foot before the other, time and time again
To see what I've never seen before
Ah! If that were life and nothing more!
To wander the Earth and only explore
from sea to sea and shore to shore
And as I'd wander, I'd dream of a lass
who'd treat me fairly and fill my glass

when I've run dry of sweet, white wine
as I scribble down line after line
describing the people and places I've seen
Ah! If only life could be many a dream
and many a place to wander from and to
If I could do as I choose, that's what I might do

If I were to do just as I wish
I'd sup on many a sumptuous dish
in many an exotic, enchanting land
prepared by many a talented hand
I'd write many an interesting, informative book
and draw many a drawing on which you could look
I'd love many a lovely and sensitive girl
in every corner of this wide world
I'd sail out to the most distant of heights
Out to the stars, even those beyond sight
I'd climb the mountains high and walk the valleys low
Swim the rivers swift and wade brooks, so slow
I'd hike desolate trails and tend billowing sails
and sleep in the deserts where coyotes wail
I'd ride on horseback through the Great Divide
There'd be nothing from me that Nature could hide
I'd be an explorer on a lonely trail
I'd be a hobo riding a railroad's rail
I'd be everything that a person could be
I might even think of a new thing or three
I'd find a way to harness the force of the seas
I'd find a way to cure each and every disease
and bring Peace and Freedom to all, me and you
If I could do as I wish
        that I'd surely do!

DREAMS REVISITED

They are hopes and plans for tomorrow
They are easy and make you feel free
They're desires and fondest wishes
for times that are yet to be

VERTIGO

Out of control
    the world spins 'round and 'round
making you feel
    like someone stole the ground
and left you to fall
    endlessly through space
reaching for walls
    grasping for a place
The world has no bottom
    and no place to stand
when vertigo has you
    within its command

THE DARK SNARLING BEAST

Sitting here feeling a little lost and lonesome
    in a life of my own design and choosing
Yesterday I felt so dizzy and confused
    It felt like I was living just for losing

I wasn't sure who to turn to
    So, I turned to no one
        I stood with all the pain held inside
As I watched the fog roll
    out over the ocean
        and felt my emotion's lowest tide

I hadn't felt so low for such a very long time
    I thought I had left those days behind
But, once again, I was reminded of how I used to feel
    And that's a part of me I try not to find

I was longing for companionship
I was longing for my brothers
who are living their own lives back east
I was needing a sense of family
I was needing a sense of love
I was needing to slay the dark snarling beast

The dark snarling beast that I know as depression
who waits in hidden corners to be found
Whose heart is as dark as the depths of space
Whose soul is as cold as the ground

Whose red eyes glow like the coals of a fire
when a breeze blows its ashes to the wind
A beast you can slay a thousand times
who finds its way back to you again

And it's the same old beast
You know it when it comes
There's no need to look it straight in the eyes
You can feel it in the room
You can feel its cool embrace
It never has to sneak up in disguise

It always makes itself a most unwelcome guest
Its chilling touch is, at once, unmistakable
It'll sink its curled claws into anyone's heart
whose spirit's human, frail, and breakable

It's haunting enough when it comes to you at night
putting its grip upon you without warning
But, what's worse is when you think
sleep has washed it away
and you wake to find it there in the morning

And, in time, you let me grab you
by your throat
and you laugh as my dagger sinks in
But you always win
you dark, snarling bastard
for you know that you'll be back again

THE FINE LINE

If you find yourself in a place
where you could not even begin
to count the stars
  Look up!
    Lay on your back
    and look up
    at the heavens
  Imagine the distance
Beyond beyond

Look up!
See the shooting stars
The steady path of a satellite
The wanderings of unexplained things

Reflections
  Comets
    Meteorite showers
  Listen to the silence
Feel the depth of space
  Absorb the multitude
    The pinpoints of light
      Each a sun

What you are seeing is the edge
  A ceiling
that is someone else's floor
  A door
to the beyond

And what is within that beyond
  that infinite space
    we seldom look at
  but always
take for granted?

Oh, a quick glance
  now and then
for the position of the sun
  or a look at the clouds
or a peek at the moon

But, how many contemplate it?
How many feel it?
How many allow their minds
to wander and explore
that limitless territory?
That wonder of wonders
which knows no bounds?

How many suns?
How many planets
surrounding those suns?
How many moons
surrounding those planets?

I'll not live to know
but I'll live to wonder
and always wonder:
Who's out there
beyond the beyond?
Whose floor is my ceiling?
Who's out there?

And here I sit
on a very fragile and fine line
The fine line of existence
The orbit of our planet
Earth

Tilted in one direction
the Mother is cold and wicked
Tilted in another direction
she is warm and soothing
but walking a high wire
on the edge of survival

Take a fraction of the distance
between her and the sun
a very small fraction
and move her
by that small fraction
closer or farther
from the sun

A small fraction closer
and her seas would boil

Her ice caps would melt
 Antartica would rise
The continents would flood
 as rivers swell
and overflow

A small fraction farther
 and who could roam the Earth?
The musk oxen and caribou
 would migrate to the equator
  The Earth
   One solid mass
  Ice and permafrost
 The oceans, frozen
The world, one blanket of white

A fine line it is!
 By design or mere coincidence?
  Pure, cosmic coincidence?

How many other civilizations of chance
 float around out there
  beyond beyond?
 How many others orbit a star
on the fine line of existence?

I find it hard to believe
 that so much exists!
I find it harder to believe
 that only we exist
The only ones to witness the wonder
 of a sky full of stars
that reach beyond our imagination

Who else is out there
 walking the fine line
  Who else?

Moon
  you touch me
    tease me
  bathe me in warmth
and your soft light
  Cradle my head
    carress my limbs
  soothe me in silence
and hold me tight

Moon
  Relax me
    Take me
  Remind me of passions
not felt in the day
  Take me to places
    where I've not been
  Make me float
so far away

Moon
  you touch me
    tease me
  Each minute of pleasure
has hours within
  Cradle my head
    Close my eyes
  Let me see you
glow again

I NEVER HAVE LIED TO YOU

I may not tell you everything
  but what I do tell you
    is true
    That way
  I can always say
I never have lied to you

BLACKBERRIES, BLACKBERRIES

Blackberries, blackberries
  out in my back yard
springing up from the ground
  that is so dry and hard
Crawling up the fence
  Spreading out at my feet
The green turns to red
  then to black
    Fresh and sweet

Blackberries, blackberries
  shining in the sun
I'll eat you all
  before summer is done
with vanilla ice cream
  I'll place you in a bowl
Satisfied, I'll not be
  'til I've eaten
    the whole

Blackberries, blackberries
  your leaves wave and worn
that I may get stuck
  by a sharp, nasty thorn
But I'll bear your cuts
  your scratches and scrapes
to place fresh blackberries
  on my
    dinner plate

BREAD IS BREAD

Bread is bread
  on that you can rely
just as water is water
  and sky is sky
And if you were to ask me
  I'd surely reply
that you are you
  and I am I

FIVE SPICE CHICKEN
(At Mekong)

Five spice chicken
  rice and coffee
Live Handel
  Bach and Vivaldi
make for a calm
  and pleasant night
with tomorrow
  and its dreams
    almost in sight

ICE CREAM

I heard my belly bellow
  and my waist begin to scream
    when I looked down
  at that great big bowl
of mocha fudge ice cream

And my soul said:
  "Go ahead, buddy
    You deserve the treat"
As my tongue said:
  "Yeah, c'mon, c'mon
    What are you waiting for?
    Let's eat!!!"

TWIST THE KNIFE

If I could look into your eyes
If I could hold your hand in mine
If I could smell your hair
  Feel the warmth
    and softness of your skin

If I could feel your weight lean against me
If I could hear your peaceful laughter
If I could taste your warm, wet kisses
  Close my eyes
    and feel your fire burn
  I would see a new tomorrow
You would bring it to me
  through your very being
    You need not try
  It would just happen
by the very nature of the moment

I would cherish that moment
  and any others
    you would allow me to have
always a little afraid of the fact
  that you may, in time
    take them away
  Either because you intend to
because you're teasing
  because you're testing
    or because you wish
      to twist
        the knife

THE WORM AND THE BERRY

As I watched the water wash
  an inch-worm toward the drain
I thought to myself:
  What would it hurt
    to let the worm remain?

I had seen this little creature crawl
on a berry in my bowl
and took it upon myself to condemn
this poor little fellow's soul

Condemn it for what?
Some minute morsel
that it innocently ate?
I turned off the water
and thought for a moment
by then
it was far too late

IT'S NOT EASY

It's not easy for you to find yourself
or say exactly what you mean
It's not easy for you to find someone
on whom you can always lean
Who understands what you're feeling
and what you are going through
The things that make you tick
The reasons why you are you

It's not easy for you to be yourself
when some don't see eye to eye
When they don't see what you are doing
or understand why you try
When they don't believe in dreaming
or finding a better way
When they think that all you can be
is all that you are today

It's not easy for us to live this life
Everyday is another trial
Sometimes it's so hard to find a laugh
Sometimes it's so hard to smile
But, this is all that we have
Make the best of it, year by year
Speaking strictly for myself:
I'm so happy that I am here

KNOWLEDGE

To some people strength is money
To some it's the ivory tower
Violence is but ignorance
Only knowledge
is true power

LISTEN TO YOUR HEART

I never was one
to hide away from the sun
now my work
keeps me in
all day

I never was one
when the day was done
to go home
read a book
and stay

But time changes things
and the changes time brings
can sometimes
sneak up
and surprise

Yes, time changes things
and the changes time brings
makes your life
flash in front
of your eyes

But that doesn't stop me
(and it never will)
from sitting on top
of a pine covered hill
Seeing the silence
and feeling the peace
of a river as it rolls
its way to the seas

And like that river
  I don't know where I'm going
   'til I come around the next bend
And like that river
  I don't know where I'm flowing
   But I feel I have a message to send

A message rolled up in a bottle
  Corked and floating
   On its way out to sea
Bobbing and swirling
  Tossing and turning
   Floating, so helplessly free

   And in that bottle
    would be a message
     written from me to who?
   Nothing profound
    that would move the Earth
     But, still, every word would ring true

   And on that note
    these words would be written
    in my unruly hand
   These few words of simplicity
    for someone to understand:

   Before your life can start
    you should listen to your heart
   When old and new ways part
    always listen to your heart

   Try to understand
    Be understanding
     and try to be understood

   Never walk away
    unless you know
     that you did all that you could

   Do not harm others or yourself
    and never rely on anyone else
   Be slow to borrow
    and fast to pay debt
   and if you haven't heard enough from me yet:

Love your family
and choose your friends
Heal old wounds
and make ammends
One day, find love
and stay in love
Don't let it fall apart
Stay happy and healthy
Believe in your dreams
and listen
to your heart

YOUR JOURNEY HAS BEGUN

Even the best laid plans
can run aground sometimes
Don't get yourself caught up
in self-made rage
When you can't see the way
or find the word that rhymes
Take a few steps back
and reinvent that stage

Don't let it get you down
Anger cannot help you see
It will only place a curtain
before your eyes
Only with a calm mind
and thinking patiently
will you find the whos and whens
and wheres and whys

Anger and frustration
are even worse than being idle
But, being idle
will, of course, get nothing done
Your hands must find the reins
and attach them to the bridle
It is then
that your journey has begun

Lazy full moon
   hanging over my head
The sun did its job
   and has gone off to bed
   A city of lights
      comes alive

Most are at home
   in favorite seats
while aimless souls struggle
   through stumbling streets
      digging through trash
         to survive

Spring breezes cool
   Love starts to simmer
as days grow longer
   and nights become trimmer
      City sky stars
         strain to shine

Summer brings love
   Love leaves you warm
Promise and hope
   spark a passionate storm
      Raindrops of tears
         or of wine

Faithful, true sun
   works long summer hours
to bring love and leisure
   green trees and bright flowers
      but never demands
         one more dime
      while that lazy full moon
   hides away
from time to time

All in all
  a total mish-mash
    of written unorganized noise
that, I suppose
  someone, someplace
    somewhere out there enjoys

I suppose
  they had their lessons
    and went to the finest schools
But their works
  always sound like a clutter
    of audible text book rules

They give you
  nothing memorable
    nor anything to hum
And I'm always quite relieved
  when it's over with
    and done

I seldom hear something with feeling
  from the heart
    or eternally moving
Give me the power of Beethoven
  or the magic
    of Mozart soothing

Maybe I'm not open enough
  and maybe
    I'm old-fashioned
But I'd rather hear something
  that stirs my soul
    with magic
      spirit
        and passion

GREETINGS FROM SAN FRANCISCO

Greetings from San Francisco
  to wherever you are out there
Here I am, with my feet propped up
  sitting back in my rocking chair
looking for words hidden under rocks
  Plucking others from the air
Thinking of times that have gone by
  They've gone, but I know not where

Greetings from San Francisco
  To wherever you may be
I hope you're healthy and prospering
  and living happily
And that every once in a while
  a thought crosses your mind of me
We haven't forgotten each other
  though we've drifted apart at sea

Greetings from San Francisco
  to wherever you are today
I hope we run into each other sometime
  somewhere along the way
and have a minute to grab a cup
  in some sidewalk cafe
to catch up on all that's happened
  since we have gone astray

Greetings from San Francisco
  This poem will have to do
if, perhaps, I never have the chance
  to again run into you
But it's really such a small world
  Things happen out of the blue
But, if not, there's an understanding
  between friends this happens to

THE PERFECT WORD

I'm not sure
 if it's a blessing or a curse
 to learn this skill
 of creating verse
 To find the perfect word
 can sometimes be worse
 than looking for something
in a woman's purse

WHAT SHOULD I WRITE?

I don't know what I should write tonight
 Somedays, time flies so fast
One moment, tomorrow is waiting for you
 and the next, it is already past

And you think to yourself: I have so much to say
 A thousand things, don't be absurd
And, although you search
 for those thousands of things
 you cannot find one single word

UNINSPIRED

Loneliness, depression
 Being broke
 or feeling tired
are among the many things
 that can leave you
 uninspired

LAST YEAR'S CALENDAR

Last year's calendar is still on the wall
and here it is the end of February
that's all

The days slip right through my fingers so fast
A new one is here
before I've thought of the last

There is no time to pretend anymore
There is no time to hide
behind the door

The time has come to reveal my soul
I'll not be content
peeking through the key hole

The time has come for me to reveal
All I've done in the past
is create and conceal

And it's time for me to show my wares
as I hope that somebody out there cares
to want to hear me
again and again
or to see me perform, every now and then

I've run out of excuses
There's none left to burn
I feel it's all right
I feel it's my turn
I couldn't live with myself
nor could I die
knowing that I didn't give it a try

A LONG DAY'S NIGHT

I have to clean up the kitchen
I have to sweep up the floor
The oven has been looking as if
it's never been cleaned before

The tabletops need dusted off
Books are scattered everywhere
And several unfinished projects
lie about here and there

There are letters that need to be written
and books that need to be read
And it's probably more than a little too late
to be thinking of making my bed

There are papers that need to be organized
and dishes left in the sink
There are several things that I haven't done
But the bills are paid, I think

Ah! But this soft chair feels so good
and this hot tea makes me warm
I'm snug here, settled in for the night
Let the weather rage and storm

The dishes will be there tomorrow
and the books aren't going anywhere
I've had a long day, I'm putting my feet up
and saying: 'So what! I don't care!'

I suppose I could try to straighten things up
and make it look as if I care
But another cup of tea
sounds better to me
if I could get myself out of this chair!

UNSOLICITED SLEEP

Droopy eyed, I sit
  not wanting to sleep
    or drift into thoughts
      too taxing or deep

With eyelids of lead
and fist against chin
  my head drops
    jerks up
      then
drops down again

A yawn and a stretch
  I twist in my chair
    keeping slumber from trying
      to take me where
rest wraps me up
  in a veil of peace
    A velvety blanket
      of starlit fleece
where worries and burdens
  seldom will tease
    Where stress and tension
      and pressures
        all ease

Sweet sleep
  Kind reliever
    Do not take me just yet
The sky is just dimming
  The sun has not set

Let me have what is left
  of this day nearly gone
Then, you'll have what is left
  of my time before dawn

YOU MAY NOT BE A SAINT

You may not be a saint
  or look like a movie star
and you may not have a diamond
            for a brain

But if your life is a complaint
  you'll be no more
    than what you are
  and you'll waste away
the time that does remain

PERSONAL SATISFACTION

Today I woke up
  with a better understanding
    of the world that surrounds me
I'm not saying
  that I have all the answers
    I'm not saying that I found me

What I did find
  is that fame and fortune
    may be quite an attraction
But, there's something more important than both
  and that's personal satisfaction

I ONLY SEE ONE PURPOSE

Today I didn't stumble on
  anything I would call profound
Nothing that made me want to scream or shout

Another day is gone
  The sun has slipped below the ground
and the shining stars above have all come out

Today has passed me by
  I'll try to capture what I can
of what's left of this quiet night before me

All I can do is try
  and that's a key part of the plan
to bring to life these dreams to write a story

You can write your life story, if you try
  You needn't be of a special breed
and you need not be within your years of youth

For, as the years pass by
  you know more of what you need
and you've a better understanding of the truth

And I only see one purpose
  for these years
    that lay before me
to learn and dream
  to touch and feel
    and write
  my own life story

HUNGER

We must search for new ways
  to ease the silent thunder
of an uncaring killer
  that is known as hunger
To whom it matters not
  whose life it takes
whose belly it swells
  or whose spirit it breaks

We must search for new ways
  to hold back the tide
These waves of starvation
  where millions have died
treading life's waters
  and gasping for breath
Living skeletons living
  a slow, painful death

We must try to quiet the children's cries
who live beneath the same blue skies
We must show them
    that there can be better days
We must continue, today and tomorrow
to conquer hunger, its pain and sorrow
We must strive to search
    for new and better ways

WHAT A GUY!

What a guy!
  What can I say?
You have this humble
  kind of quiet way
of dealing with
  the world around you
Your interests
  and all that does surround you

When you do something
    you do it right
with patience and humor
    that keeps things light
You taught me how
    to teach myself
and to depend on me
    more than anyone else

Though you've never been a guy
    that says very much
Your actions show the world
    that you're in touch
You always seem to have the answer
    just in reach
whether you're hard at work
    or walking down the beach

You taught me to run
    and jump right in
and that it's the only way
    to learn how to swim
That lesson still helps
    when I approach a task
If you don't know
    look it up
        If you can't find it
        ask

You've influenced much
    of this person in me
        My insight
        My music
        My poetry

And I'll take a moment
    just to say
        Have a wonderful
        Father's Day!

THE OLD RED BOMBER
(To Wendall Quan and Bobby Salvador)

I sold the old Red Bomber today
My first car
That ugly little critter
One hundred seventy-six thousand miles
and a million memories

I charged up San Francisco hills
and stalled her out
in the middle of an intersection
on my first ride home
Felt like a fool
But, hey, I'd never driven a stick before
Give me an 'A' for effort, will you?
I did

I learned about mechanics with her
from my brothers
whether I liked it or not
I was always short on cash
to do otherwise
And who can afford real mechanics
but the rich
and the mechanically inept?

I cursed and I loved that thing
A true love-hate relationship
that car and I had
She died out on me once
at ten o'clock on a sunday night
on the Oakland Bay bridge
I-was-not-happy

She was ugly and faded and worn
Her roof leaked
Rotted the carpet on the passenger's side
Smelled like a swamp on warm, rainy days
Luckily, there aren't many warm, rainy days
in San Francisco
Rainy days, yes
Warm, rainy days?
Not often

And when you don't have a garage
and the weekend is the only free time
that you have to work on her
and it's one of those rain-all-weekend
sort of San Francisco weekends
the hate part of the relationship
was in full bloom

How many busted knuckles
from wrenches slipping?
How many aching backs
from leaning into the engine compartment
on a cold, gray, rainy, San Francisco sunday?
How many shivering moments
crawling under her on the wet pavement?
Too many
Far too many

But, she got me around for six years
and she was ten when I bought her
Seven hundred and fifty dollars
from a fellow named Wendall
She was the ugliest car I ever saw
but she got me around
She and I and my brother George
went clear up to Mount Shasta
Mount Lassen, too
Not to mention Yosemite
and Lake Tahoe

Yeah, that old girl got us around
Not without many a mysterious
mechanical moment
I can guarantee you that
Many a mechanical mystery
found by patience or luck
and then...VA-ROOMMM..she started
and purred like a kitten again
She had a nice purrrrrrrr...
But...Oooo! Weee!...was she ugly!
Rusted out roof
Three hubcaps
You had to sort of guess
at what color she was
It was sort of red

But, she got me around
and she taught me alot
A high school boy named Bobby came by
Asked what I wanted for it
I said 'Three hundred'
He said 'I'll take it'
It was his first car
and he liked her so much
that I dropped it to two-fifty

Four cylinders
Four speed
Four doors
but not to be
forgotten...
my old Red Bomber

A CHANCE MEETING

I saw you walk out of a store today
    It was down in Chinatown
I wasn't there for any particular reason
    I was only out driving around

I watched as you stepped to the side of the street
    I hadn't seen you in quite awhile
But I remembered the softness of your voice
    and the sweetness of your smile

I called your name as you stepped across
    as a breeze played with your hair
You turned your head and our eyes met again
    Was some of the magic still there?

We waved to eachother
    and exchanged a few words
        A simple gesture of greeting
As once again the paths
    of our lives crossed
        in a brief and fleeting
            chance meeting

Foggy beach
Walking down a foggy beach
All my dreams just out of reach
and a hush falling over me

Hills of pine
Walking through lush hills of pine
Trying to find what could be mine
in life and fantasy

Summer days
The wonder of summer days
The way the sunlight plays
in ripples on the lake

Maple trees
The red glow of maple trees
when autumn's on the breeze
and winter's in its wake

Summer love
The magic of summer love
with a billion stars above
Feeling life and time stand still

Winter winds
Distant, bitter winter winds
Causing summer love to thin
from an everlasting thrill

April rains
Spring again brings April rains
Chasing frost from window panes
Bringing life back to the ground

Thrown and tossed
Sometimes feeling thrown and tossed
Trying to find what I have lost
and lose some of what I found
And here I am again
Yes, here I am again

BRING DOWN THE BROWN SUGAR

Bring down the brown sugar
  The cinnamon and oats
The scarves and mittens
  and warm overcoats

Boil up the water
  to make steaming tea
and add to the warmth
  within you and me

For here comes upon us
  another winter day
Christmas is here
  with New Year's on its way

Let us give thanks
  for all we have and give
Let us be kind and warm
  so long as we live

Let us hope all children
  of the world will be free
to live and dream and hope
  and love like you and me

Let us hope that all hunger
  will soon disappear
to be replaced by laughter
  fulfillment and cheer

Let us raise our glasses
  and drink a toast here
to a very merry Christmas
  and a happy New Year!

Well, there it is!
  And there it goes!
    It's the last day of the year
    Another old one on its way out
and another new one is here

Now, what promise shall I make to myself?
  One that I have broken before?
Maybe I should promise myself
  not to promise myself anymore

What new plans can I put off?
  What excuses can I use to wait?
I have so much ambition to plan
  and even more to procrastinate!

Well, there it is!
  And there it goes!
    Will I treat this year the same way?
    When will I get it through my head
that the future is today?

I'M SO TIRED

I'm so tired
  All I do is stretch and yawn
I'm so tired
  I should be to sleep by dawn
I'm so tired
  and feeling so worn
that I'll sleep like a baby
  straight through to the morn

THREE TIMES TODAY

A hummingbird stopped by
  to visit me
    three times today
  to sit on a rock
flutter its wings
  in water
    and fly away

It sat on a branch
  and looked at me
    no doubt wondering:
      What is that?
I wonder what it thought of my shoes
  my jacket
    and my hat

Twice
  it flew away and returned
    to this little waterfall
      The water
    rushing all around
  this little bird
so small

Hovering here
  hovering there
    then swiftly darting away
A hummingbird stopped by
  to visit me
    three times today

I walk the shore
  windblown by the sea
    balanced on the edge
      of life's trilogy

A wind so wild
  it hurts the ears
    abuses one's hair
      and causes warm tears
to trickle their way
  down windblown cheek
    like a babbling brook
      a river, or creek

Tall breakers roar
  and rush to the shore
    to fall to their knees
    and bow before
the shifting sands
  and lands beyond
    who with the sky
      all form a bond

A bond 'tween Earth
  and all life there
    Life of the land
  the water
and air

I walk the shore
  windblown by the sea
    balanced on the edge
      of life's trilogy

SMALL CHANGE ON THE DRESSER
(TO TOM WAITS)

Throwing small change on the dresser
  he looks into the dusty mirror
and fingers a few of the photos
  tucked into the cracked wooden frame
There's dear ol' Ma, God bless 'er
  I'm glad she doesn't know I'm here
And this one in the fancy clothes
  Christ, I can't remember her name

Was it Matilda, Maureen, or Melissa?
  I don't know, it might've been Mandy
Ah, whoever you were, sweet lass
  I hope you're living good in a suburb
If you were here right now, I'd kiss ya
  and pour you a shot of brandy
into my cleanest dirty glass
  as we sat out talkin' on the curb

We could watch the cars go by
  and the dogs runnin' into the street
lookin' lost, scared, and confused
  and not sure of which way to go
We could see pigeons scurry and fly
  as they scramble for something to eat
tossed down by an old man, looking amused
  as he shuffles, stiffly and slow

We could take a bus to Barney's Beanery
  Have us a chili and a cold beer
down on Santa Monica Boulevard
  near the joint with all the pancakes
Yeah, we could take in all the scenery
  The sights to see and sounds to hear
Pick up a magazine or a postcard
  Anything and everything, whatever it takes

We could walk down dazzlin' Hollywood
  look at the sidewalk with all the stars
and I'll tell ya 'bout how I had a chance
  to work with DeNiro and Keitel

And with the night feelin' young and good
we could dodge between moving cars
and go to my favorite place to dance
I'll close my eyes and find it by smell

Yes, I'll find it by smell
'cos they make the best meals
you've eaten in all your days
The drinks are cool, the lights are low
and the band plays it sassy and hot
We can play it by ear
and see how it feels
as the evening slowly strays
We can stick around here or we could go
Time is all we've really got

We could go back over to my place...

Suddlenly, he looked up into the mirror
and saw the last trace of a smile fade
as his weathered face turned to stone
He turned away to stare into space
let the fantasy disappear
and listened to the torn, yellowed window shade
beat itself in the breeze, all alone

He walked over and sat on the edge of the bed
that was home to last winter's mouse
Beneath, the dust was a blanket of gray
and the old springs creaked and complained
Scenes of horror were haunting his head
A dream career and a little dream house
He said he'd do it all one day
but only memories of wishing remained

In his head, the house was drawn and designed
He had walked through each room and hall
He once felt the warmth of a fire he'd make
He once smelled the smells that filled it
Somehow, somewhere on the way he resigned
bowed his head, and gave up on it all
In all his life, his greatest mistake
was waiting for someone to build it

And there he sits, alone in the glare

of a bar's red neon light
to live with himself and linger
through another long, lonely night
waiting for the world to turn around
once more, all the way
when he'll throw small change
on the dresser again
at the end
of another long day

WHEN YOU'RE AROUND

I could look at your face for hours
and never tire of its beauty
I could listen to your laughter
and never tire of its sound
I could watch your graceful movements
and never lose them from my memory
I'll never tire of the feelings
I feel
when you're around

YOUR VOICE

If I were to take
all soothing sounds
and had to make one choice
Before the waves
or the waterfall
I would choose
your voice

FRIENDSHIP

Friendship is to be concerned
and friendship is for caring
Friendship is for listening
and friendship is for sharing
Friendship is one who understands
Friendship is a helping hand
Friendship is silence without strain
Friendship is someone who'll heal the pain
Friendship is hours of conversation
sharing thoughts without reservation
Friendship is forgiving
Friendship is for living
Friendship is a part
of each and every heart
Friendship is far below the skin
Friendship is somewhere deep within
Friendship is something money cannot measure
Friendship is one of life's
most precious treasures

OUT IN THE RAIN

Look out in the rain
You'll find romance there
when you have an umbrella
two lovers can share

BALLET

Graceful feet and swaying arms
practice and devotion
brings ballet to the stage
honoring music, mind, and motion

THE SAME OLD STUFF

I'm always doing the same old stuff
  I need to do something new
Something exciting and different
  Something romantic too

I need to see something
  I haven't seen
    Do something
      I haven't done
to work with these goals I dream about
  as I watch the setting sun

And tomorrow will be a better day
  if I follow this type of plan:
Research your interests
  Believe in yourself
    and continue to say
      " I can! "

DECEMBER TWENTY-THREE

Here it is December twenty-three
as I try to keep a promise I made to me
I swore with every day I age
I'd place a poem upon a page
Whether it be simple or deep
Whether it be shallow or steep
Whether it be lovely or lame
I must write it down, just the same

Writing to merely loosen the rust
  To take the creaking from my brain
These phrases may fade into dust
  or may be read from California to Maine
In Tokyo or Taipei or Timbuktu
  In England, Australia, or Spain
In a meadow under a sky of blue
  or by a fire, away from the rain
And if, by chance, you get to read these lines
  I hope a phrase or two you'll retain
For as I drift along through this life of mine
  I hope I've many a chance to refrain

ODE TO THE POET

Could anything else ever be
  quite as fun as writing poetry?
Bringing to life line after line
  of anything that comes into mind
To write the ridiculous and scribe the sublime
  bouncing with rhythm and chiming with rhyme
To carve out of time word after word
  whether it be worthwhile or at best absurd
To paint a picture in groups of letters
  (I can think of a few things that might be better)
But here's to the poet, nonetheless
  who writes of love and pain and distress
Of courage and tales of adventures bold
  Visions of the future and stories of old
Of gentle maidens with long braided hair
  and young men who wander without a care
Tales of the sea, tales of the land
  Tales they create with mind and hand
Called, at times, the nation's jewels
  but are mostly called nothing but lazy fools
who lie about all day in meadows, by streams
  lost in their silly, romantic dreams
Writing of love or the flight of an eagle
  (Are you sure having this much fun isn't illegal?)
Whether the poet be a diamond or rust
  may their wonder and words never crumble to dust
For they offer us wisdom and they offer escape
  and the word without the poet
    would be like wine
      without the grape

THERE WAS A TIME

There was a time
  when I stared out of windows
    There was a time
      when I paced the floor
    But now I find
  I can't waste my time
waiting around anymore

There was a time
  I was lost in depression
    always dragging my feet
      on the ground
    But now I see
  that is not for me
There is so much more to be found

With head up and mind clear
  I must take action now
    even though
      there's a bit I must borrow
    Though I'll go into debt
  there are things I must get
to build a better tomorrow

There was a time
  when these plans were dreams
    Transparent
      and floating in air
    There was a time when I
  thought I'd live and die
without seeing them get anywhere

NOTHING MORE

Nothing more
  have I to say
So, I'm going to put
  my pen away

GIVE A GIFT OF POETRY TO A FRIEND

If you enjoyed this collection of poetry and
would like to have a copy sent to a friend...
we'll do it for you. And we'll include a
card with your personal greeting on it. IT'S
EASY!!! SATISFACTION GUARANTEED!

- - - - - - - - - - CUT HERE - - - - - - - - -

WHISPERING SANDS / JACK SHINER

Check one: Softcover_____ Hardcover_____
Ship to:
    Name_____
    Street_____Apt____
    City_____ST____ZIP_____
Your Greeting:_____

Check one: Softcover_____ Hardcover_____
Ship to:
    Name_____
    Street_____Apt____
    City_____ST____ZIP_____
Your Greeting:_____

COMPLETE ORDER   TOTAL
    Softcover _____ copies @ $ 6.95 = ___.___
    Hardcover _____ copies @ $11.95 = ___.___
                   Sub-total=$___.___
    California residents add 6% tax = ___.___
    Shipping chg @ $1.00 per address= ___.___
                    TOTAL $___.___

Send check or money order and coupon to:
    Stargazer Music & Publishing
    P O Box 34189-B
    San Francisco, CA 94134-0189

Allow 4 to 6 weeks for delivery

DID YOU BORROW THIS BOOK?

If you enjoyed this collection of poetry and borrowed it from a friend or your library.... we'd like to make a copy available for you to own.

Jack Shiner's WHISPERING SANDS and Other Poems is available in both a cloth hardcover edition and a quality softcover edition. Both editions are printed on natural white 60 lb acid free paper to ensure lasting quality. Your satisfaction is guaranteed.

- - - - - - - - - - CUT HERE - - - - - - - - - -

WHISPERING SANDS / JACK SHINER

Ship to:
Name_____

Street_____Apt_____

City_____ST____ZIP_____

COMPLETE ORDER   TOTAL
    Softcover _____ copies @ $ 6.95 = ___.___
    Hardcover _____ copies @ $11.95 = ___.___
                Sub-total $___.___
California residents add 6% tax = ___.___
Shipping $1.00 for first book
   $0.50 for each additional book= ___.___
                TOTAL $___.___

Send check or money order and coupon to:
    Stargazer Music & Publishing
    P O Box 34189-B
    San Francisco, CA 94134-0189

Allow 4 to 6 weeks for delivery